Psycho-Analytic Insight and Relationships

A Kleinian Approach
by Isca Salzberger-Witt

Psycho-therapist
Tavistock Clinic, London

ROUTLEDGE

LONDON and NEW YORK

First published 1970
by Routledge & Kegan Paul Ltd.,
Reprinted 1973, 1975, 1981, 1984 and 1986

Reprinted in 1988, 1991 and 1993 by
Routledge
11 New Fetter Lane, London EC4P 4EE
29 West 35th Street, New York, NY 10001

Printed in Great Britain by
St Edmundsbury Press Ltd, Bury St Edmunds, Suffolk

British Library Cataloguing in Publication Data available

Library of Congress Cataloging in Publication Data also available

ISBN 0 415 03446 9

Contents

III: Gaining insight and applying it in the casework relationship

Acknowledgments

When I think to whom I owe thanks for being in the position to write this book, I realize that I can only mention a few amongst many.

First and foremost my gratitude is to my parents. They have filled me with a sense of wonder and the wish to understand and link experience in a meaningful way.

The book itself is an acknowledgment of Sigmund Freud's, Karl Abraham's and Melanie Klein's work.

I owe my knowledge and personal experience of psychoanalysis to many valued teachers. I would mention three in particular whose personal example and rich understanding remain my inspiration: Dr W. R. Bion, the late Dr S. Davidson and Dr D. Meltzer. Dr Meltzer was kind enough to read the manuscript and make valuable suggestions.

I am deeply indebted to Mrs Martha Harris for her most helpful advice and encouragement at various steps of writing. My thanks are due to the Editor for his constructive suggestions and corrections.

A group of senior caseworkers have provided most of the case material. To all of them and particularly their leader, Miss Jean Leared, I am grateful for sharing their casework experience and knowledge and offering constructive criticism. I thank those child psychotherapists and psychiatrists who have allowed me to use examples from their work; and Miss E. Richards for helping to correct proofs.

Finally, I could not have written at all were it not for the tolerance and support of my husband and children.

I.S.-W.

Introduction

The purpose of this book is to indicate some of the ways in which Sigmund Freud's psycho-analytic theories as developed further by Melanie Klein, can help social workers in understanding their clients and their relationships with them.

There are at least two ways of setting about this task. One is to state the theory first and then see which parts of it are most relevant to social work. Alternatively, we might take the caseworker-client relationship as our starting point, examine it in the light of insights gained in the field of psycho-analysis and study the theory subsequently. The second approach is the one that I have chosen. I have not adhered rigidly to it, however, and case material will often be found interspersed with theory and vice versa.

Psycho-analysis is still a very young science and our present knowledge of the complex working of the mind is limited and in need of constant testing and further development. There are those who oppose or disregard the findings of psycho-analysis altogether, and there are different schools of thought within the psycho-analytic field. The theories here presented are the ones that seem to me, within the limitations of our present knowledge, to best fit the phenomena they try to explain and to make clinical sense. Theories are, after all, only attempts at explaining a set of phenomena and they are valuable in so far as they appear to fit the facts and are helpful in practice. My endeavour is to do no more than to show how they have been arrived at and to put them forward in a way that I hope will be comprehensible to an intelligent and open-minded reader. No previous knowledge of psycho-analytic terms will be assumed.

The term psycho-analysis has two different meanings. It is used to denote: first, a body of knowledge and theories about mental and emotional states, and secondly, a particular method of therapeutic treatment. While the insights gained in psycho-analytic practice are of great relevance to other disciplines especially in the educational, medical and social field, the psycho-analytic method clearly is not. It is the task of each profession to work out in which way they can most usefully and appropriately apply the insights first gained from the psycho-analytic study of the personality.

To apply one field of study to another requires either an intimate knowledge of both, or co-operation between representatives of the two disciplines. Although my training in Kleinian psycho-analysis and child psychotherapy was preceded by one in social science and casework, my experience of field work was inadequate for the purpose. I felt the need to learn from social workers, and to explore the relevance of psycho-analytic insights in social work in a dialogue with them. A small group of experienced caseworkers drawn from different fields was therefore invited to meet me for discussions about their cases and those of their students. The examples and problems they brought, my thoughts about these and our joint discussions, together with my psycho-analytic knowledge form the basis of this book.

Practically all the case material has been taken from work with individuals. The knowledge gained from detailed study of one person and his relationship with others, helps us in understanding the more complex interactions within groups. Although the application to group and community situations has not been spelt out in any detail, it is hoped that the psycho-analytic insights to be discussed will be seen to be relevant in this area of work also.

The book is divided into three parts. In Section I, we shall look at some of the feelings with which client and caseworker approach their relationship and at such concepts as transference, the importance of phantasy and the inherent conflict between love and hate. In Section II we shall study different kinds of anxieties, and defences against them, and the way these, and envy, affect our relationships. I shall try to indicate how Melanie Klein's work derives from Sigmund Freud's and Karl Abraham's and take into consideration some of the contributions to our understanding made by the present generation of Kleinian psycho-analysts. In Section III we shall consider factors which facilitate the caseworker's understanding of the client and make the relationship therapeutic. We shall also discuss some of the emotional burdens and pressures to which social workers are exposed.

I am very aware of the limitations of this book and know that many important subjects have been inadequately covered or been left out altogether. It is hoped that the book will be a stimulation to further reading and lead caseworkers to consider their experience in the light of what we have discussed and so gain insights on the basis of their own experience.

I
Aspects of a relationship

1

Feelings the caseworker brings
to the relationship with the client

Although we have to use shorthand terms like 'case-worker' and 'client', I am always thinking of people or a particular person needing help and a particular individual offering help. For the sake of clarity, I shall refer to the caseworker as 'she' and the client as 'he' except where I give case material, and there the sex of the actual person will be indicated.

The first meeting of caseworker and client is a new experience for both; they come together eager, though in different ways, to find out about each other. Although it is a new experience, their relationship and particularly their initial contact, will be greatly influenced by the attitude each partner brings to the situation.

It is important for the caseworker to be aware of her feelings so that they do not stand in the way of her really getting to know her client as an individual. Otherwise she may be so preoccupied by her eagerness to be helpful, by what her supervisor or Head of Department will say, or busy proving to herself how successful she is, that these considerations overshadow the interview and distort her perception and reactions. If these feelings can be worked over beforehand and kept in check if they occur during the interview, the worker will be freer to observe and take in what is going on here and now. The worker must also rid herself of preconceived notions about her client from one interview to the next. Every time is a new beginning, and while there is shared knowledge and experience, the worker needs to be free to see her client afresh, to allow another facet of her client's personality to come forward and permit change and development.

The expectations and fears the caseworker may have are innumerable, and depend on the particular caseworker's personality and experience as well as on the nature of the problem she is faced with. I can only mention a few common ones which I have come across.

Hopeful expectations of the caseworker

To be a helpful parent

Most caseworkers set out to be helpful and see themselves in a good parental role, *vis-à-vis* their client. Their wish to engage in social work may spring from a deep desire to repair situations and relationships but in order to achieve this aim, reparative zeal must be geared to what is realistic and of benefit to the client. 'Do-gooder' is now a term of insult, conjuring up a picture of someone rushing in, impatient to show how much good she can do, without full consideration of the needs of the person requiring help. In this extreme form it may sound ridiculous, but there is a danger, especially for the beginner, to have to *prove* to the client (and in the back of her mind to herself) that she is helpful. The need to reassure herself that she is doing something of value may drive the caseworker to give advice when she is not yet fully in possession of the facts, nor able to judge what receiving advice may mean to the client. Or she may intervene very actively in his life without defining the limits of her role and in this way mislead her client into believing that she will take on a full and active parental role rather than a professional one. The caseworker must be clear in her own mind what she can realistically offer, bearing in mind her caseload and what she can expect of herself.

To be tolerant

Because of her wish to be a helpful parent to her client, the caseworker may entertain an expectation of herself being kind, gentle and tolerant. These qualities are certainly desirable in someone entrusted with the confidence and care of human beings in need of help. But too often gentleness, kindness and tolerance, are not distinguished from an attitude which comes close to appeasing or colluding with the client's aggressive feelings and behaviour. We need to distinguish between tolerance based on the ability to acknowledge the client's feelings and being able to bear them, and being so frightened of the client's hostile behaviour and negative feelings that they have to be glossed over or excused in some way. The caseworker in the latter instance is implicitly communicating to the client: this is too bad to be acknowledged, therefore let us ignore it, call it something else or pretend it is not there. Clearly this is not tolerant at all, and the client will understand that the worker cannot stand hostility, depression, despair. If the caseworker cannot, how can the client?

Here is an example: Mrs X cancelled three appointments with a psychiatric social worker. On every occasion she offered an explanation. Once she said she missed the train, another time she did not feel very well; on the third occasion she forgot. Today she phones half an hour after she was due to come, and talks non-stop for five minutes saying that she just couldn't make it, she was going to come but decided to wait for the bread-van to call. The delivery was late and she tried to get a bus and missed the train. The caseworker sympathized with Mrs X's difficulties in having such a long way to come and asked whether she could expect her next week, offering a choice of time: Mrs X is evasive, says she will see, hopes she can make it. The worker leaves it at that. Mrs X does not come next week. Nor does she ring or write.

It is true that the caseworker was sympathetic, recognizing the external difficulties, but was she dealing with the client's feelings? No one mentioned that part of Mrs X did not want to come to the interview and that external factors were used to express inner reasons for staying away. Was the caseworker not evading the dilemma of the client who could not bring herself to the interview because she was in a state of conflict? Some verbal recognition of the difficulties, internal as well as external, might have given the client some trust in the worker's ability to understand her conflicted self and so perhaps enabled her to come. But suppose the client decided to stop treatment altogether. It would have been such a relief for her to be helped to say that she did not want to come and to experience the worker as one able to tolerate this. Otherwise she may be left with such guilt feelings at having rejected the 'kind' worker that she may find it impossible to return later when she may be more motivated to seek help.

Some caseworkers feel so guilty about losing a client that they sometimes hang on to him under any circumstances. The adult client has a share in the responsibility for his treatment and the freedom to break it off when he wants to. The caseworker might also remind herself that there are more people wanting to get help than staff to deal with them. (These considerations of course do not apply where there is a statutory obligation to keep up a contact with a caseworker such as in Probation or certain Child Care cases.)

To be understanding
By virtue of her training and experience the caseworker may feel justified in feeling that she has knowledge about human relationships which will help her in understanding her client. She needs to guard, however, against a sense

of omniscience and superiority in relation to other human beings. Acquaintance with theories about human beings does not give a key to understanding people but tends to remain unintegrated and to be applied indiscriminately unless such knowledge has become part of one's living experience. Clients are not embodied theories. They are human beings, each with their own complicated and unique personality though they have basic patterns of relationships similar to others.

Here is an example of the danger of applying knowledge indiscriminately. A medical social worker was dealing with a case of encopresis in a boy of seven. In taking the social history she learnt that the mother of the boy had recently started a part-time job. At once she was convinced that this accounted for the boy's encopresis, that he was deprived and insecure because of his mother's absence. In vain the mother tried to explain that she was always at home when the child returned from school, nor did she work in school holidays. The fact that the mother worked was *ipso facto* interpreted as deprivation and as the reason for the child's illness. This prevented the worker from looking for deeper causes for the child's complaint.

There are two separate misconceptions here: first, that in every case it is wrong and harmful for the child's mother to work; secondly, that the cause of an emotional disturbance lies invariably in the parent. There are two partners to every relationship and all we know at the beginning is that something has gone wrong in the delicate interaction between them. We cannot say what or why until we know much more about each of the partners and the way they interact. Theories are formulated to help us organize our thoughts about the interaction between people and the different parts within the personality, but in no two persons are the manifestations and constellations exactly the same. Each case provides us with an opportunity to discover something new.

7

The caseworker's fears

Let us now look at some of the fears which beset the caseworker meeting her client. Some anxieties are part and parcel of the price we pay for engaging in such responsible work; for the beginner there is the additional guilt of knowing that the client will credit her with authority and knowledge by virtue of her holding a position in the agency. Will she be able to understand the client's feelings? Will she not do harm to her client? If she allows herself to be receptive will she be invaded by the problems put before her, overwhelmed like the client by depression or fear? How is she to cope with silences in an interview? None of these anxieties can be lightly dismissed. The fact that they are experienced shows that the student is in touch with her feelings and trying to deal with them. Supervision is essential, not to do away with such anxieties but to afford a check on whether the caseworker's own problems are interfering and distorting the work process.

There is room only to take up three of the fears I have often come across, while some others will be dealt with in Section III. Students sometimes express a fear that in exploring their client's feelings, they are 'digging into' and 'doing harm'. Related to this is the notion that psychological insight means looking 'with X-ray eyes' into someone's mind. Each of these statements denotes an aggressive act, something like forcing one's way into the other person without his knowledge, against his wishes and interest. This is not the place to go into the childhood sources of such anxieties. This will be discussed in Section II. Here I want to question these assumptions.

Probing and digging into the past

Casework students sometimes say that they do not like 'probing' and 'digging into' the client's past. Indeed, they would be wrong to attempt to do so. I think that the assumption is based on a misconception. The client comes because he is *at present* in some difficulty. There is therefore no need to dig into the past; the past is only relevant in so far as it is still active and influencing him today. It is therefore something traceable in the here and now, although it may have its roots far back in childhood. Perhaps it is the caseworker's fear of the on-going emotional relationship to herself that makes her want to explore the past. Here is an example. A young man tells the worker shortly before her holiday that he hates saying goodbye and feels angry at having recently been left by a friend 'high and dry'. It is correct to assume that these feelings were first experienced in babyhood when he might have felt unsupported by a mother's arm and dry in the mouth when she went away; but the client is saying this *now* because he experiences the separation from the caseworker as being left with his problem, unsupported, in a state of needing more mental feeding. The client is bringing the baby part of himself that operates at that moment in relation to the caseworker.

Doing harm

The fear of doing harm may have various sources: the caseworker may be afraid of what forces she is unleashing when she allows her client's feelings to emerge and afraid of things getting out of control. If these feelings are so readily available to the client—and in casework we do not usually deal with deeply unconscious feelings—one would suppose it is far safer for them to be brought out in the caseworker's presence than burst out somewhere else where they may do more harm. The caseworker might ask herself whether she is afraid of her own reactions and finds some emotions too disturbing and painful or whether she is afraid of not being able to control the client.

The caseworker may fear that she will hurt the client if she says something inappropriate. Unless clients are very disturbed they are not so vulnerable that a wrong remark would upset their whole balance.

She may feel that she is causing suffering by allowing the client to experience painful feelings; but in fact a client will find great relief if he is able to share such feelings. The caseworker's ability to stand emotional pain and to be tolerant will enable the client to incorporate and identify with her and so become more tolerant of himself and others.

To look with X-ray eyes

Does psychological insight really enable us to look into somebody's mind like a machine taking an X-ray picture? This fear is often linked to the idea that the student's personality is transparent to her supervisor. The student will soon discover that the situation in reality is vastly different. At best, we understand only a fraction of what is going on, and we depend at every step on the co-operation of the client. It is both a limitation and an essential condition of the work that it is a joint enterprise and can be hindered, virtually stopped, or broken off by the client at any time. (Compare example on page 5 of this chapter.) It is true, however, that a person's behaviour, facial expression, voice, manner, posture, etc. tell us a good deal about him, providing clues to those prepared to look and listen. One does not necessarily have to be trained to have such perception and draw inferences from it. Mothers often have acute intuition about their young baby's states of mind and on the basis of this respond to his needs. Such psychological closeness occurs when the mother has sufficiently worked through her own infantile anxieties and is therefore able to accept and carry those of her baby. What we need, in order to understand our clients better, is not a mechanical aid to looking and listening, but the ability to be sensitively aware of what it is like to be that other human being, in the effort to overcome the limitations of separateness and differences.

2

Feelings the client brings to the relationship

Hopeful expectations

Long before the client meets the caseworker he has ideas about the kind of person he wants her to be and what she is to do for him. The nature of these expectations depends on the client's maturity. In everyone, however, there are some hopes which are unfulfilled, and every new venture tends to arouse our ideal expectations. It is as if we were saying 'this time it is going to be different; this person will give me all I ever longed for'. In as far as our expectations are ideal they are unattainable; in as far as they are reasonable, they have a chance of being met.

To rid himself of pain

Basically, the ideal the client hopes for is that the caseworker will take away all pain. To this end the client may tell the worker what she should do: e.g. 'get me a house, then my wife will look after the kids properly, and I won't go to the pub any more'. Alternatively, he may treat the caseworker as if she was an oracle: 'Tell us what to do!' 'Tell me who's right!'/ 'I'll do anything you say.' 'You know what's best.' These attitudes are met with again and again, both in individual work and in groups. The pressure to get the caseworker to give answers and to make decisions arises from the avoidance of emotional pain connected with not-knowing, uncertainty; and self-hate and guilt when things go wrong. If the caseworker does not fall in with such demands, she may be told that she gives nothing worthwhile and become the object of hostility.

Another way of ridding himself of his troubles is to pour them out, with no effort to try and understand them. A social worker will say 'he told me too much in the first interview, he won't come back'. Such intuition implies that the client has used the caseworker as a dustbin, has massively evacuated his problems into her and is likely to become frightened in case the worker will put it all back, reproach him, or make him feel ashamed.

To find someone to help carry the burden
If the client is looking for someone temporarily to carry his anxieties, to share his burden and to help him towards finding a solution, this can become the basis of a realistically helpful relationship. 'You are the first person who has taken the trouble to listen to me, who is really interested, who cares', are expressions of gratitude and show how great is the human need to find someone who is a good listener, capable of carrying anxiety—and how rarely this need is met.

To be loved
To be loved is every human being's most ardent desire. At the deepest level this means being loved as we are, with all our faults and shortcomings. This requires that someone should understand us in the widest sense of the term and yet not reject us. It is such understanding that the more mature part of the client is striving for. Yet there is always the doubt whether it is possible to be loved if the truth were known, and hence the worker may find

herself being seduced into a relationship based on mutual admiration of each other's nice qualities. If this happens she must ask herself what has happened to the bad aspects of the client and herself. If, because of her own need to be loved and admired, the caseworker allows herself to be idealized, she is not helping the client to face the inevitable frustrations and disappointments of reality. On the contrary, the client will all the more concentrate his anger on someone outside, e.g. the marriage partner.

Fears the client comes with

To be blamed

As the client comes for help because there has been a failure in dealing with himself, his family or the outer world, the notion that he will be criticized is near at hand. He may be full of self-reproaches, 'it's all my fault' (which is unlikely to be so) or adopt a belligerent attitude. 'It's no good investigating me, you will find nothing in my family that accounts for Janet's behaviour' was the opening remark of a mother to the psychiatric social worker. Implicit in this statement is the client's assumption that the purpose of the interview was to attach blame and that it would end in a moral indictment. Feelings of guilt may lead to the withholding of important information or blaming someone else: 'I am sure it is the school'; 'It all started since she has been going out with that boy'. The client tends to pick on some simple external reason to explain what he dare not or cannot understand. There is a positive aspect to this, however, namely the belief that if the true cause can be discovered some answer might be found.

To be punished

Guilt and a moralistic outlook lead to fear of punishment. Child Care Officers come across children who feel so guilty and responsible for the breakdown of their parents' marriage that they expect their foster-parents to be wicked people to whom they are sent for punishment. Probation Officers, as representatives of authority, have a particular problem here. If the probationer has been treated in a punishing way before, this will make him even more sensitive to any hint of punitive attitude in the Probation Officer. The offender may behave in a way designed to provoke the Probation Officer to become angry and punitive, and then feel justified in believing him to be as irrational and uncontrolled as he is himself.

To be abandoned
Once the client has been able to trust the caseworker enough to tell her about himself he may feel very vulnerable. His hopes have been raised and he fears he will be abandoned by her before his troubles have been sorted out. It may be difficult for the caseworker to appreciate the full weight of her commitment to her client from the beginning. Through the very act of seeing him, she is putting herself forward as a person who accepts responsibility for feelings of trust and dependence. She must remember that the client brings not primarily the adult but the infantile aspects of his personality that are in need of help. As with his parents in the past, he is liable to interpret her actions as if they all refer to him. If she hands him on, is it because his problems are so serious that she cannot cope with them? If she goes on holiday does she not care? If she leaves her job has he undermined her ability to work? These are but a few of the many anxieties that may beset the client.

3

Transference and counter-transference

Transference and its implications for casework

We have seen that caseworker and client alike have expectations about each other even before they meet. Such ideas are based on their past patterns of relationships and we therefore say that they are *transferred* to the present.

Such *transferences* of feelings influence the new relationship in important ways. As R. Gosling (1968) has pointed out, they affect the way we (a) perceive; (b) interpret the new situations and (c) influence it; for our behaviour, in terms of our assumptions, tends to elicit a response in the partner(s) which fits in with our expectations. An example of (a) was the woman who felt so responsible for her child's problems that she saw the caseworker as highly critical of her, someone who would blame her. An example of (b) is the client who interprets his caseworker's absence as the result of the excessive demands he made on her. An example of (c) is the young offender who, expecting punishment, behaves in such a provocative way to his Probation Officer, that the latter finally does in fact respond in an aggressive and punitive way.

It is most important, therefore, for the caseworker to be aware of the nature of transferred feelings. Knowing that such feelings *are transferred* from the past may help her to look at the situation more objectively. The deep feelings of love, hatred and dependence which the client experiences towards her may have less to do with her personal worth, than finding himself in a relationship where such feelings are reactivated. Secondly, such awareness will help the caseworker to resist colluding with or being manipulated by the client to fit in with unrealistic expectations whether they be of someone bad or ideal. In this way, instead of being encouraged to act out his feelings, the client is forced to become aware of them, to compare them to the reality of the situation and to deal with his frustrations.

The concept of transference

We owe the discovery of the phenomena of transference to Sigmund Freud (1895). When he found that hysterical female patients tended to fall in love with their physician, he first regarded this as a nuisance and hindrance to the work of analysis. But he had the brilliance subsequently to arrive at the conclusion that what was happening was that the patient was re-experiencing feelings that he had had previously towards someone else, e.g. the girl towards her father. Such feelings had given rise to conflict, had been suppressed, and found an outlet in the hysterical symptom. In the psycho-analytic setting, they surfaced again. Freud later found that all kinds of earlier conflicts involving hate, jealousy, rivalry, etc. entered into the relationship with the analyst. 'A whole series of psychological experiences are revived, not as belonging to the past, but as applying to the physician at the present moment (1905, p. 116). Such repetitions made it possible for earlier conflicts to be understood and undergo change. It also enabled Freud, to a large extent, to reconstruct the patient's past. On the basis of many adult analyses, Freud was able to arrive at hypotheses about the sexual development of children. Direct observation of children has since proved these to be correct.

Through Melanie Klein's work (1952) the concept of transference has extended in two directions. First, she widened it to include not only repressed conflicts but the whole range of earlier emotions which enter into a relationship. Secondly, it has deepened in the sense that Klein's analysis of children showed that what is transferred are both more grown up elements and all the infantile feeling states which persist right through life.

It is in the Kleinian sense that I have applied transference in the foregoing chapters. We shall later need to examine the nature of the 'child and baby feelings' existing within the adult, and trace their roots to infancy.

Counter-transference

The caseworker, like the client, brings to the situation expectations, fears and problems transferred from the past. For instance, she may see in the client before her some aspect of her mother and consequently feel herself still to be in the position of a little girl, unable to help this adult. Or, faced with a couple, her problems of jealousy in relation to her parents may incline her to support one against the other. She may be over-inquisitive, motivated less by the wish to understand and be concerned about her client than driven by the need to intrude into other people's private life as she might have once wanted to enter into the secret life of the parents from which she was excluded, or she may be so frightened of such inclinations that her natural curiosity is inhibited.

There is a common tendency for workers to side with children against their parents because of the wish to blame one's own parents for whatever has gone wrong in one's life. This is, of course, particularly so if the child in fact appears to be rejected or the mother expresses hatred for her child, in spite of the caseworker's theoretical acceptance of a non-critical attitude! We need to dis-associate ourselves sufficiently to be able to ask: 'Why does this woman feel like this about this particular child?', and appreciate the mother's difficulties. If we do, we may find that the mother's hostile or even murderous feelings are not so alien to our nature after all, for we harbour in ourselves similar hidden feelings towards siblings or un-acceptable childish parts of ourselves. Sometimes a parti-cular problem so closely corresponds to the worker's own, that she is either blind to it or alternatively gets over-involved.

The term 'counter-transference' was coined to denote feelings which the worker transfers from the past and inappropriately applies to the client or his problem. Super-vision and self-examination are important to check whether clients in general, or particular clients or specific problems tend to trigger off in the caseworker her own unsolved problems. In so far as they do, this will distort her perception and interfere with her interaction with the client.

In recent years, the term counter-transference has also been used in a different sense: namely, to describe the reaction set off in the worker as a result of being recep-tive to the *client's* transferred feelings. These emotions, in so far as they correctly mirror the client's, are a most helpful guide to understanding. Often, they give us a clue to the feelings which have remained unexpressed. For instance, a client may evoke great concern in us as if the child in him was crying out for maternal care although he may tell us repeatedly that he doesn't want any help. Or, for instance, feeling in despair after a client left may be the only clue, that behind the client's outburst of anger there is a hopeless, miserable part of himself. After a holiday, a child sat for weeks behind books apparently completely rejecting me and the treatment. This was her way of communicating to me what she had felt I had done to her in the holiday, and how terrible it was not to be able to get in touch.

It becomes pertinent therefore to ask oneself: what does this person make me feel like? and what does this tell me about him, about the nature of the relationship and about the effect he has on others? Further, we need to question ourselves whether this is valid intuition, a response in terms of what the client is communicating or whether we are reacting in terms of what *we* are putting into the situation. Such questioning can lead to greater understanding, of oneself, of the client and of the nature of the 'here and now' relationship.

4
Phantasy

Another way of talking about the ideas and feelings with which we invest any new situation is to say that we have *phantasies* about it, about ourselves, about others, about the nature of our relationship and the relationships between others. Such phantasies are partly transferred from the past but continue to be modified and developed in the present, in response to inner and outer stimuli.

Phantasy and the caseworker

We have already (in Chapter 1) looked at the caseworker's feelings about herself and her client. Let us now consider the worker's changing perception of herself, her work and her colleagues. One week, for instance, she may feel that she possesses outstanding ability, that she has scored brilliant successes, and that her colleagues do not accord her the recognition that is her due. Such phantasies about herself are likely to affect the way she holds herself, the confident way she walks, her whole manner and expression. At another time, the same caseworker may feel that she is a failure, no help to anyone, not worthy of the confidence others place in her. At yet another moment in time she may feel reasonably satisfied with herself and her situation. These views, although contradicting one another, must all be part of a composite picture which the caseworker has of herself. Most of us are subject to such mood swings, though the frequency and extent of change varies from one individual to the other. Variations in one's experience of oneself can appear without change in external circumstances.

If we are completely dominated by our phantasies, then no evidence to the contrary is likely to make much difference to our feeling state. We call a person psychotic who is most of the time dominated by his phantasies to the extent of being quite out of touch with reality. The ordinary person finds some evidence in the external world which lends substance to his phantasies, i.e. he selects from his environment those elements which fit with his preconceived notions. Let us assume that the social worker, already feeling undervalued, comes to the office and hears some disparaging remark about herself, or finds that someone else has been chosen for a more senior position. Such events, sometimes of a quite trivial nature, can be used to confirm and strengthen her phantasy of being unfairly treated. She may overlook other evidence which does not accord with her phantasy. If, on the other hand, she had just been in a self-critical frame of mind, the same situation might make her feel very guilty, confirm her doubts about herself and convince her that she is a failure. Yet again, had she been feeling generally liked and confident in herself, she might be able to consider what was valid in the criticism, perhaps momentarily experience guilt; and regard not being promoted with no more than a passing regret and a twinge of envy of her more fortunate colleague.

Phantasy and reality

Let us now assume that the attitudes described above are characteristic of three *different* people. The over-confident social worker, who permanently feels undervalued by her colleagues, is by her aggressive self-righteousness and overbearing manner, likely to annoy others and they may in fact want to keep her down. The one who feels inferior, on the other hand, will not be able to fight for her rights, or do so in a way, or at a time, when she is unlikely to succeed. Similarly, a mother, doubtful of the quality of the milk she is offering to her baby, will handle the baby in a clumsy way and present her nipple so awkwardly that the baby may well reject it.

Thus, our behaviour in terms of our phantasy expectations influences those around us, and in this way we help to shape our environment in the image of our phantasies. This also accounts for the fact that people often end up in situations which bear a strong resemblance to one another. For instance, they may have one disappointing love affair after another, each following the same kind of pattern, because they select a partner who fits in with the unconscious phantasy expectations.

The opposite, however, is also true: that the environment, hostile or friendly, sparks off corresponding phantasies in us. But even when our perception is accurate (i.e. we are actually being unfairly treated and hated, or loved and appreciated), phantasies tend to give the experience a halo-effect, to lead to an exaggeration in one direction or another. Yet most people most of the time can respond to a situation that is sufficiently different from their expectations. For instance, a parent fearing the caseworker's disapproval but finding that she is sympathetic and non-judgmental, can then begin to look at his feelings of guilt, i.e. the *reason* for his phantasy, rather than go on expecting blame. This is why it is so very important not to fit in with the phantasy-role in which we are cast, but yet to allow the phantasies to come to the fore. For only then can they be examined in the light of inner and outer reality. If a child who fears punishment is constantly smacked, he feels that his parents *are* as bad as he imagined, but if he is treated with firm tolerance, he is presented with something better than his frightening phantasies. In this way the environment can confirm or alleviate fear, strengthen or undermine hopes. Environmental factors become even more pertinent when they are seen as interacting with the individual's phantasies.

Sometimes people say 'It's only phantasy' or 'It's just imaginary, there is no truth in it'. Such an attitude to phantasy, which as we have seen is part and parcel of our mental life, may make us think that the most vital thing is always to check up on whether the facts bear out what the client reports. Of course, diagnostically, this may be very important. For instance, we would want to know whether a client's life is being threatened by his relatives or whether what he tells us is his phantasy. Indeed we would need to know in order to take appropriate action. Yet even if the client's relatives are not endangering his life, it is important to realize that he feels they are, and that the phantasy may express for him a terrifying *internal reality*. From the point of view of *understanding* the client, it is *his* perception of reality which concerns us.

Perhaps we are so eager to stick to consciousness and reality because we tend to associate phantasy with madness, someone living in a 'world of phantasy', and of our own frightening phantasies. Indeed, phantasy may serve a defensive function, an escape from reality or a massive distortion of reality. But it has a far wider meaning in psycho-analytic usage: it is a way of describing the kind of imagery and feelings that are set off by an experience. We may describe an experience in a factual way or elaborate it, using our phantasy indeed to highlight an aspect of reality.

Some years ago Walt Disney produced a film called 'Fantasia' which showed the kind of visual images and ideas evoked in an artist by listening to some masterpieces of music. We might think of phantasies in a similar way: as ideas, images, thoughts with which we respond to inner and outer stimuli. Indeed, we regard individuals who are out of touch with their phantasy as impoverished, boring, too prosaic, while we usually admire the richness of phantasy expressed by artists and children at play. Scientists, too, of course, if they are to get beyond purely mechanistic enquiry and observation need to be capable of leaps of imagination so as to formulate hypotheses, discover causes and connections and penetrate further into the unknown.

Phantasy is thus a part of every individual's mental life. What distinguishes the ill from the less disturbed is the *nature* of the phantasies and how far they are in tune with external reality.

The concept of unconscious phantasy

Imagination, daydreams, phantasies about ourselves and others, all these form but the top layer of a substream of on-going phantasy-life of which we remain largely unaware.

When Breuer and Freud worked on the problem of hysteria, they found that patients under hypnosis related phantasies which they did not recall when awake (1893-1895). Yet, these phantasies, excluded from consciousness, had most powerful effects on the individual. They affected his moods, behaviour and even brought about changes in physical functioning (e.g. trembling, palpitation, partial paralysis). Such findings led Freud subsequently to arrive at some of his most fundamental conclusions. First, that there exists a whole world of ideas of which we are normally not conscious, and further that the *unconscious part of our mind* exerts a very great influence on us. Secondly, that part of the personality sets up a *resistance* against many of these ideas coming into consciousness and therefore they tended to remain unconscious. They were inadmissible because they were felt by the conscious part of the personality to be bad, forbidden or out of keeping with the dictates of our knowledge of reality. Later Freud found that these ideas welled up in dreams and could also be reached by the patient verbalizing whatever came into his mind without censoring his thoughts.

Another feature of these unconscious thoughts was later to reveal itself. At first, Freud thought his hysterical patients had actually been sexually assaulted or seduced; but he came to see that the accounts of such events which the patients reported gave a picture of what the patient *felt* had happened or had wanted to happen, i.e. it was an event as elaborated by the patient's unconscious phantasy. When Melanie Klein undertook child analysis, she found that the child's play also did not correctly mirror the actions of his family or herself, rather it showed what the child made of other people and real life situations. (E.g. 'The Psychological Foundations of Child Analysis' 1926.) His perceptions were coloured by his phantasies, which in turn were coloured by his prevailing emotional attitude and feelings towards others. For instance, a child driven by jealousy of his parents' 'togetherness' may in phantasy (conscious or unconscious) attack and dirty them. This may lead to the idea that sex is dirty, disgusting, frightening. Such ideas, in spite of intellectual knowledge to the contrary, may remain and influence his attitude to sex and to the body as such, in childhood and adulthood.

Mrs Klein's work with young children enabled her to penetrate deeply into the content of phantasy-life. In the safety of the analytic treatment situation, the child was able to express in play and action how in phantasy he felt himself to interact with others. She found that: (a) each activity, sensation, impulse, had a phantasy representation; (b) these phantasies were experienced as concrete happenings; (c) many of the phantasies in the child's mind —and also existent in the adult's—were extremely primitive, quite out of keeping with the more grown-up part of his personality. On the basis of these findings she hypothesized that *phantasy is the mental expression of impulse* and is operative from birth; and that the infant, from the beginning of life, has a primitive relationship to the mother based on the phantasies arising from physical and emotional needs.

The body-mind link

One of the startling findings made by Freud and Breuer was, as we saw, that phantasies could cause severe physical symptoms. This opened the way to understanding that it was possible to suffer physical pain and severe discomforts without organic changes having taken place. These feelings were real enough, and therefore simple dismissal of them as due to 'malingering', or 'laziness', or 'just put on', and telling the person that he was just imagining them, did not meet the real situation. The individual was in fact using his body as the vehicle for expressing powerful but deeply unconscious phantasies.

Sometimes the person is quite unaware of any underlying anxiety and only experiences the physical phenomena. The unconscious phantasies may nevertheless result in short-term effects such as vomiting or stomach pain in a 'work shy' person or a school-phobic child. Long-term functional changes may bring about organic damage as, e.g., in some cases of peptic ulcer and hypertension. (Of course, it works the other way too: physical illness and pain can evoke in us very frightening and depressing phantasies.) On the other hand, most people are aware that there is a link between insomnia and worry and that an emotional upset can cause a mother to lose her breast milk. Yet, the *detailed phantasies* underlying the emotional disturbance tend not to be within our perceptual reach. At other times we may feel our fears to be inappropriate, e.g., we may tell ourselves that there is no particular danger attached to standing in a lift, yet be unable to control sweat and terror as the doors close. Similarly, we may panic and suffer physical side-effects 'for no reason' when we travel by train, speak in public or any number of other situations. Yet analysis has shown that our fears make sense in terms of the unconscious, primitive phantasies associated with such events. Also, that when these phantasies can be experienced in a relationship, come into consciousness, and be understood, the physical symptoms may disappear and anxieties diminish.

Introjection, projection and the internal world

There is another aspect of the body/mind link to which we must turn our attention. We speak about mental functioning in terms which involve physical processes. We speak of *'taking in'* knowledge and good experience, of *'distasteful'* ideas, of *'digesting'* facts, of *'pouring out'* our troubles, of *'pushing'* unwanted thoughts out of our mind as if they were physical entities. This is more than colourful speech. We are expressing our phantasy that mental and emotional happenings ·can be incorporated and expelled. This leads us also to phantasies about what we 'contain'. The elated person may feel full of knowledge, full of good experiences, full of love, and the depressed person feel empty and full of rubbish. We feel that an 'inner voice' tells us to do or not to do something.

Freud (1923) thought that the child came to acquire a conscience and moral standards (a super-ego) by absorbing, i.e., psychologically introjecting his parents' explicit and implicit demands. Freud felt that this happened around the age of four or five as a result of the child's fear and admiration for the parent of his own sex; that is to say that the boy, for instance, dealt with his rivalry of the father by identifying with his ideals and also with his moral strictures. Freud showed that such identification based on introjection of precepts, laws and ideas of the important figures in our environment, such as parents, teachers, religious leaders and political thinkers, made us behave like them and hold similar views. Their ideas became internalized by the process of introjection, and part of the mental structure of the individual.

Karl Abraham (1924) attached great significance to the psychological processes of introjection/incorporation and also to its opposite, projection/expulsion of feeling. He held that the individual constantly interacts with others in this way. Incorporation is the basis of all learning. It is therefore possible, for instance, for the client to introject a tolerant and understanding caseworker, and this can become a pattern of mothering with which the client can identify in his relationship to his child and the child-parts of himself.

The opposite process also takes place: we expel, project unwanted feelings, hate and destructiveness in its various forms. But as Susan Isaacs (1952) says 'mental mechanisms are but an abstraction for what the individual experiences as a concrete phantasy'. The destructive feelings are then felt to be inside someone else; at first mother, father, siblings, later in life they are attributed to all kinds of people, or to particular political, social or racial groups. The aggressive parts could be said to be always seeking an object to put themselves into. Sometimes they find a suitable object, someone who fits in with the preconceived pattern, sometimes it is done indiscriminately.

Abraham hypothesized that these processes originated in infancy and are associated with the baby's sensation of taking in food, holding and feeling it inside him, and expelling, pushing out unwanted products. He considered that phantasy accompanied all physical acts of the infant, and that the baby related to the mother in terms of the digestive process of incorporation and expulsion. He saw in this process of interchange, of introjection and projection, and reintrojection, the basis of character formation; for what the baby takes in and introjects becomes part of his personality. (This process as we have seen continues throughout life.) In this way Abraham drew attention to the importance of the early relationship and linked psychic and somatic happenings. As we have seen, in phantasy this primitive link continues to exist so that we conceive of mental happenings even in adulthood in terms of concrete physical events and conversely attach emotional significance to physical ones.

Mrs Klein was able to substantiate Abraham's hypothesis about the nature of the early infantile relationship and her work added a wealth of information about the content of the phantasy life of young children. This has led to an enriched understanding of the infantile elements of the psyche and also made it possible to attempt the treatment of severely disturbed and psychotic patients. For in her view, in the earliest months the basis is laid for a sound or unsound mental structure and this deeply influences later development and the nature of subsequent relationships.

The feelings of love and hate (influenced also by external circumstances) lead to hopeful or frightening phantasies. These phantasies then influence perception so that we tend to take in again a reality that is either more hopeful or affected by our fearful phantasies. In this way a vicious circle is set up, which seriously affects subsequent external relationships. Moreover, anxieties arising from frightening phantasies continue to exist in what Klein has called 'the internal world' and the child will be driven to more and more defensive measures to cope with pressing fears. The good experiences which counteract these phantasies can, however, help to alleviate the situation and start off a more benign circle. It is this situation which results to some extent in the gradual modification of phantasies in accordance with external reality.

Primitive phantasies, however, continue to remain in the depth of the mind and can erupt in times of stress at any later period. All of us contain an internal phantasy world which may be either an attempt creatively to bind together, or else deny and cut apart, aspects of internal and external reality. Thus day- or night-dreams may be constructive efforts to work over the happenings of the day or they may be a way of fastening on to something pleasant, a wish-fulfilment which tries to eliminate the painful external reality and the painful inner tensions it has set up. Equally, there are artists who depict either only the lovely or the ugly side of things, while the truly creative genius shows the tragedy of 'Beauty and the Beast' in its eternal struggle. (Compare Segal, 1956, and A. Stokes and D. Meltzer 1963.)

5

Love, hate and conflict

When we considered some of the feelings which case-worker and client bring to a relationship, we were able to group them under the two headings of hopes and fears. Hopes related to the expectation of constructive, enriching relationships, while fears centred around destructive, revengeful interaction. Both sets of feelings are present in all of us, though we may become aware of them at different moments of time or as related to different people, as if they existed quite separately. When they do come together we call our attitude one of ambivalence. These expectations are, as has been stated, largely transferred from past experience, but we also saw that our perception of past and present alike is influenced by our phantasy and that phantasy in turn is highly coloured by unconscious motivation, i.e. by emotional impulse or drives. What is the nature of these inborn emotional impulses?

The polarity of inborn drives

All through his life's work, Freud grappled with the problem of defining the nature of inborn drives. His theoretical formulations derived as always from his clinical work. What forced itself upon his attention was the constant dynamic struggle which appeared to be pulling the individual hither and thither. This can be seen very clearly in obsessional patients who can never make up their mind. Conflict is universal. Freud found it existed in the unconscious itself and in his view this was the cause of anxiety and neurosis. It was as if one part of the personality was constantly in opposition to another. This led him to assume that there was an inherent dualism in man's nature.

I shall not attempt to trace Freud's developing thinking about these opposing inborn forces. Suffice it to say that he discarded several times the views that he had previously held; for whenever clinical experience did not bear out his assumptions, he was ready to change them. Towards the end of his life, his observation of the repetition compulsion, i.e. the tendency to repeat over and over again painful as well as pleasurable experiences, and his studies of sadism, i.e. pleasure in inflicting pain, and masochism, i.e. pleasure derived from suffering pain, led him to the assumption that there was something at work within human nature which, so to speak, worked against the individual's own interest. In *Beyond the Pleasure Principle* (1920) he put forward a daring new hypothesis about the duality of inborn drives, which presented a far deeper chasm between them than stated before. He differentiated between the Sexual Instincts in their widest sense, Eros, or the Life Instinct aiming for union, constructivity, creativity and integration, and Thanatos, the Aggressive or Death Instinct whose aim was destruction and disintegration, ultimately of the organism itself. He assumed that this Aggressive Instinct existed in the first place within the individual but that the organism at once defended itself against internal destructiveness by directing it outwards. It thus became discernible only in the form of sadism, negativism and aggression. Freud thought that a part of this aggressive drive became fused with the life force, the loving component of the personality, and mitigated by it. This would provide the element of aggressive forcefulness necessary for growth and progress. What is fused could however become defused and lead to such unabated murderousness as is seen in wanton acts of cruelty and self-destructiveness.

Karl Abraham accepted Freud's view of an inherent struggle between love and hate. He found in the analysis of severely depressed adults that they harboured phantasies which seemed to him to stem from the early oral phase of development. He hypothesized that under the impact of love the baby took in, internalized a loving breast (and other aspects of the mother), while when he was under the sway of hate or anger he introjected a destroyed, bitten one. Such internalization on the basis of hatred resulting in phantasies about destroyed objects in the mind, he saw to be at the root of severe mental disturbances as well as accounting for some character disorders.

Melanie Klein corroborated Freud's and Abraham's findings. Powerful hating impulses bent on destruction of others and the self existed in the very young child side by side with loving impulses. The child's mind seemed dominated by phantasies of, on the one hand, highly ideal figures resembling fairy godmothers and magicians, and, on the other, by terrifying ones like monsters and witches. As these bore little resemblance to the actual parents, it was further evidence that the child's perception and phantasies were strongly affected by primitive love and hate. The primitive nature of some of these phantasies which refer to parts of the body, parts of the person rather than whole people, confirmed to her that they stemmed from a very early stage of development. From this she hypothesized that from the beginning of life loving and hating phantasies attach themselves to the important people in the baby's life (or rather those parts of their bodies and mental functioning which become meaningful through sensory perception). These formed the forerunners of what we later call social relationships, although parts of the mother may be at the very beginning experienced as if they were parts of himself and only gradually perceived as separate. However, because of the need to dissociate himself from destructive feelings and 'put them outside', there was an impetus to recognize the existence of something (or somebody) separate from himself.

The need to project inherent destructiveness and the anxieties arising from it made the baby dependent on the mother to 'take them away' and the relief thus gained generally promoted the further development of the relationship. Bad feelings are not the only ones to be projected, for we also invest others with loving feelings. The whole complexity of human relationships, our desire to be loved, our wish for and fear of a close relationship can all be seen to have their origin in our need inert at the beginning of our life, for someone to supply our psychic as well as for our physical needs, to protect us from destructiveness outside and inside and to strengthen our potential for life and love.

The quality of the baby's relationship was thus seen not only to depend on the environment, but also on the infant's own contribution, basically on his innate endowment, the relative strength of love and hate. Detailed observations of infants bear out the fact that they vary greatly in their behaviour right from the start (compare, e.g. Middlemore 1941). This may be due to distress at birth or prenatal experience, about which we know as yet very little. But even taking these factors into consideration, amongst infants with apparently similar experiences, there are some who are more outgoing and receptive to the mother's feeding and loving handling, are able to put up with waiting more easily, and respond more readily to being comforted when distressed; we would presume that such infants have a greater inborn capacity for love. Others need far more attention, coaxing, comforting, as if destructive phantasies more easily gained the upper hand.

Yet others cry incessantly and no amount of patience and help seems to satisfy them fully, as if bad feelings were generally dominant; and yet another kind of infant appears apathetic and apparently lacking in a strong drive for life.

Whatever the inborn balance of love and hate, the duality of inborn drives results in a mental life perpetually in a state of flux and engaged in conflict with others and within itself. The anxieties which arise from such conflict will be discussed in Section II.

From our everyday observation of human behaviour, seeing the constant disruption of social relationships by hatred, jealously, rivalry, greed and other destructive feelings, our despair and efforts to establish more constructive relationships, we might suppose that we would have no difficulty in acknowledging a constant struggle between love and hate. Yet the assumption of an aggressive drive, inherent in human nature and not merely a response to provocation or a not good enough environment, has met with the strongest opposition. We seem to want to cling to the belief in our ultimate goodness and to be reluctant to take back our own share of hatred, adding to what may in fact be a very destructive situation. But the alternative is to see aggressive drives only in others and continue to battle with them in a spirit of self-righteousness that furthers quarrel and warfare, or alternatively to submit to bullying and collude with cruelty and deviousness. On the other hand, knowledge of the destructive elements in ourselves and others leads to clearer judgment, increased tolerance, supported by greater firmness and thus to the possibility of more constructive relationships.

When we consider the qualities we most admire: courage, wisdom, integrity, we implicitly acknowledge that those who possess such qualities have achieved maturity by having struggled with and being able to continue to deal with the destructive elements in their personality and that of their fellow human beings. This may make us realize that there is indeed something very positive in the inherent polarity of drives. Like the electricity sparked off by opposites, so the state of conflict produced by the interplay of love and hate creates a constant current of mental activity. It may result in disaster or standstill but when the anti-life elements destructive to development are struggled with, the outcome of such conflict may be commensurate with achievement and growth.

6

Interaction

A relationship is a two-way process in which both parties affect each other. We have looked at some of the phantasies and how they might influence the relationship. While the caseworker is bound to have problems of her own, she will want to be aware of them so that she can as far as possible control their interference in her professional work.

This is much harder in private life. When we think of the relationship between marriage-partners and particularly between parents and young children, we realize that they are so closely bound together in the most personal way that their feelings and moods constantly affect each other.

Caseworkers usually come into the life of the clients when the partners have arrived at a point of crisis or even a point of no return. She gets some, but often only a limited chance to find out how it all began. This is why detailed observation, particularly of mothers and infants is so very instructive. It gives us an opportunity to study a relationship in *status nascendi*: the process of interaction, of fitting in, the mutual adjustment that takes place between two people and the understanding that may develop. Detailed observation teaches us also how *mis-*

understanding, *mis*-fit and *mal*-adjustment come about.

Mother, baby and father

If we consider for a moment some elements of the feeding situation, we find that a series of quite complex adjustments have to take place. The mother picks up the infant, holds him in her arms and finds a comfortable position for him and herself. She places the nipple in his mouth, and this has to be at an angle and in a way that enables him to get hold of it and keep it inside. She has to produce the milk at the right moment and the baby has to learn to grip the nipple, move his jaw to stimulate the breast to produce milk, and adjust his swallowing to the speed of the milk's flow. In other words these two people, or the 'nursing couple' as Middlemore aptly calls them (1941) have to learn to get in tune with one another. This may in some cases take quite some time and require tolerance and patience. Furthermore, all these physiological processes are known to be influenced by emotional ones: we know that shock, worry, depression, may reduce or even stop the mother's supply of milk. Anger, fear, (or apathy following a difficult birth) may interfere with baby's readiness to take hold of the nipple and suck. Disturbance in one partner is communicated to the other and affects the other's moods and responses.

Here is an example. P. was a strong, healthy baby. From the start, he put up a fight whenever he was put to the breast. He seemed to want the breast, as he eagerly turned his head in search of it; yet at the point of contact he screamed or alternately would turn away from the breast after the first few sucks, struggling and crying.

The mother had no previous experience of babies. During an uneventful pregnancy she had looked forward to the birth of her first-born. So she was surprised and shocked at holding in her arms a screaming, raging, demanding baby whom she could not satisfy. It made her feel, in her unestablished role as a mother, that there was either something wrong with the baby or with her milk. If it was the baby, then what sort of baby had she produced? Was he damaged? Was he monstrously greedy? More prominent, however, were her feelings that she could not do anything right for her baby and she began to have doubts about the amount and quality of her milk.

The more anxious she became, the more her handling became inconsistent, fussy and jerky, and the baby in turn became still more excited, frustrated and so less capable of being at ease with her and of being satisfied. He cried a great deal, day and night. The mother hardly got any sleep, grew progressively more physically and emotionally exhausted, and eventually frightened and angry with the baby's inexhaustible demands.

Dynamic interaction

What we see here is the *cumulative* effect on a relationship where the two partners are caught up in a vicious circle of frustrating and anxiety-producing interaction. Luckily in this case the father remained calm and believed that his wife's worries were understandable in the circumstances. He had no doubt that his wife was the right person to feed the baby and would find a satisfactory way in time. He also helped by carrying the baby around on his shoulder and allowing the mother to get some sleep. In other words, he was able to contain the mother's and baby's anxieties, acting as a mother to the mother.

In time, the mother and baby became quieter, though the baby remained demanding, fighting and easily frightened. Imagine how difficult such a mother/baby relationship is where the mother is without a helpful partner or the baby was unwelcome in the first place! On the other hand, an originally unwanted baby may by his responsiveness and loving dependency call out maternal feelings in quite an unexpected way and a benign circle be initiated.

We see how the close physical relationship of mother and baby has a parallel in their psychic closeness. Because mother and child are so important to each other and both so vulnerable, the effect they have on one another is highly dynamic. We know that children are prone to be 'naughty' when parents are nervous, worried or pre-occupied. Babies are still more sensitive to their partner's moods and feelings which are partly transmitted through bodily contact: in the way that mother picks up and holds the baby; whether she is tense or relaxed with him, the way she speaks and looks at him. I have been told by a father of a 2½-month-old baby that sometimes when he holds his baby daughter and finds his thoughts wandering away from her, she starts whimpering. She stops crying at once when he pays attention to her. It would seem that the very attentiveness of the parent may be extremely important at even such an early stage.

Of course it is the quality of the attention which matters: whether it is an accepting and understanding one or all anxious watchfulness as in the following example:

A psychiatrist when consulted because of an infant's inability to fall asleep, noticed that the mother continually juggled her crying baby on her lap. Eventually he asked to be allowed to hold the baby while he continued talking to the mother. She said the infant made her anxious (and this made her wish to 'shake' the fear out of herself and him). After she had talked for a while the mother was amazed to find that the baby had dropped off to sleep and was lying peacefully in the doctor's arms. As in the above example the doctor was able to contain the mother's and the baby's fears and remain a protector to them both.

The family

The father's most important role at the beginning of the

child's life would seem to be that of a supporter to mother and baby. In a good relationship the father is someone in whom mother can confide her anxieties about her maternal role. Mothers are usually very vulnerable after the birth of the baby, and as well as being proud and excited, tend easily to get depressed and anxious. The father infuses hope and steadiness into the mother during the hurly-burly of the first few weeks.

The experience of a mutually satisfying feeding relationship, achieved by adjustment, and the secure framework given by parents who complement each other becomes the basis of the child's experience of a creative relationship. This will eventually become linked in his mind with the sexual union and creativity of the parents. The introjection of such a good relationship will become the foundation of his stability. The child's perception of his family is influenced on the one hand by what he brings to it, namely by his love and hate, and on the other by the actual nature of its members, as individuals related to life and related to each other. All these together will affect the internal phantasy world of relationships and shape his view of himself as an individual and as a member of the family. Later in life this will affect his relationships to bigger social groups and the founding of his own family.

Schematic presentation of interaction

To give some indication of the variety of possible interaction without taking up too much space I should like to use a schematic presentation. This involves gross oversimplification and the factors mentioned are not intended to be in any way exhaustive; furthermore it leaves out the dynamic cumulative effect briefly discussed above and the changes that come about throughout adjustment and growth. All the impulses and phantasies in the baby are assumed to be present to some extent from the beginning of life.

ASPECTS OF A RELATIONSHIP

Baby	*Mother*
(a) Inborn preconception of something good to fulfil his need, making his mouth search for and respond to breast.	Phantasies about baby prior to his birth, varying from dread of monster to hope for good or perfect baby. Balance of such phantasy is dependent on her attitude to own mother, father, young siblings, baby's father, life experiences and feelings of own worth.
(b) Capable of building phantasies round sensory experiences.	Able to enjoy body sensations in feeding and handling baby; if mother too seductive, she may over-stimulate baby's sexual feelings; if afraid of these she may keep baby at arm's length, thus encouraging a split between mind and body.
(c) In accordance with inborn strength of love, he is capable of loving phantasies; in varying degrees he is capable of being receptive to love. If he is responsive and loving, soon able to smile and engage in loving play, he evokes more love, because of his 'lovability'.	In accordance with her ability to love the baby, she is able to express love in handling, feeding, holding baby, responsive to his needs. If she is depressed, baby's loving behaviour may pull her out of her depression. If she is too depressed, she may be unable to respond to baby, depriving him of an emotionally alive and reciprocating mother. This can lead to early despair in baby and even to autism.
(d) In accordance with inborn strength of destructive drive he is capable of destructive behaviour and phantasies and in varying degrees afraid of hostile world.	In accordance with the integration of the destructive parts in herself, she is in varying degrees able to deal with such behaviour. If she is afraid of baby's aggressiveness she may set rigid limits, or be punitive, or if she denies his aggressiveness she may be unable to set limits. If she recognizes it and is unafraid she can be tolerant and firm.

Baby	*Mother*
(e) Because of his limited capacity to contain destructive feelings, he needs to project them, experiencing mother and treating her as bad.	In accordance with her feelings about her own goodness she is able or unable to bear this. If she can tolerate such projections she can allow baby to reject her without feeling too angry or depressed; she can handle baby tactfully and thus introduce differentiation between phantasy and reality. If she is not able to take projections of badness she may behave seductively or in a punitive way; or else she may get progressively anxious or depressed, thus strengthening the baby's feeling that his destructiveness is omnipotently powerful.
(f) Sensitive to hostility.	If she is hostile to the baby, or the 'baby part' of herself, rejecting of baby and confirming his fears of a hostile world.
(g) At first limited but growing perception of reality; he finds it accords with or contradicts his phantasy expectations. He gets reassurance against fears (or not); e.g. Mother's continued existence means his destructive phantasies do not kill, thus he gets an affirmation of mother's strength and his phantasies of omnipotent destructiveness are diminished.	Unless she is psychotic, by virtue of experience of living, she has more reality sense and is able to help baby to sort out phantasy from reality. Inability to do this in any particular area tends to be transmitted to the baby e.g. a phobia, or a fear of messes. Mother's sudden disappearance or death confirms that his destructiveness is capable of killing her.
(h) Drive towards growth and integration.	Depending on degree of integration in herself she is able to hold together the good and bad aspects of baby and herself. Recognizing and able/ unable to adapt to child's

ASPECTS OF A RELATIONSHIP

Baby	Mother
	growth, changing needs, skills and capacities.
(i) Needing mother to help him with mental as well as physical pain and differentiation between material and emotional need.	If mother cannot stand mental pain in baby or herself, treating all pain as physical, she encourages somatization of mental phenomena, the substitution of material provisions for emotional needs.
(j) In varying degrees capable of tolerating frustration. If totally unable, fragments all painful experiences and finally information coming from sense organs themselves—resulting in reduced perception of reality. If able to stand some frustration, can be spur to mental growth.	If in touch with baby able to judge what this particular baby can stand and mediating between him and too overwhelming frustrations. If she exposes baby to more than he can stand, this leads to increased feelings of persecution in baby. Over-protection from frustration may lead to unduly infantile character, e.g. encouraging the belief that he is entitled to special conditions of living, so that when he is not accorded them, feels he has a righteous grievance.

These are but a few of the ways in which infant/child and mother may interact. Within the range of possibilities the extreme cases stand out:

(a) A baby/child/adult so endowed with love that he is able to extract from experience whatever good it contains and use this to strengthen his trust, and is at the same time capable of overcoming frustrating experiences with a minimum of resentment.

(b) At the other end of the scale, a baby/child/adult so angry at the slightest frustration that he reacts with deep and lasting resentment and will need constant help. In extreme cases, even this is not enough, and the person becomes psychotic, or does not survive.

Looking at it from the environmental side:

(a) A mother so secure in her maternal role that she is able to stand a great deal of rejection and anger from the infant and yet remain calm and lovingly concerned.

(b) A mother so immature and rejecting any responsibility (or for a variety of reasons absent in body or mind) that the infant has to be endowed with unusual love to withstand falling into despair and apathy; in extreme cases prone to infant mortality. An equivalent outcome may result where there are frequent changes in mother figures, as with institutionalized babies or children moved from home to home.

(c) A mother so unresponsive because of her depression that she is locked within herself and unable to be receptive to messages of either love or anger from the baby. This may force the baby to withdraw into itself and seek satisfactions from his own body or material objects; autism may be one outcome.

(d) A mother using her baby as a receptacle into which she projects her confusion or own infantile conflicts and destructiveness. This may result in schizophrenia or an unhealthy symbiotic relationship.

II
Conflict, anxieties and defences

1

Persecutory anxieties and defences against them in the adult, child and infant

A frightened client

Mrs B., a thirty-four-year-old married woman with two children of school age, was referred to the Local Authority Mental Welfare Officer by her doctor following her brief stay in a Mental Hospital.

The worker found a slight, anxious-looking woman who keeps her flat very clean and neat, tastefully furnished in rather muted colours. The client says that her main trouble is that she is afraid to go out in the street. She had tried to be sensible about it but she couldn't get herself out of the house. As soon as she tries, she panics, and has an attack of dizziness and nausea. She will not allow daily papers in the house for fear that they contain accounts of war and murder. Her children play mainly outside because she cannot bear their noisiness and demands. She dislikes her father-in-law's visits, complains that he is rowdy, and she would much prefer to be 'left in peace'. When her husband is out, she is terrified of what will befall him and gets into a panic when he comes home late. She praises him for his patience with her and his placid nature (the worker got the impression of a colourless, immature young man lacking in masculinity).

Mrs B. tells the caseworker that she used to be head-strong and had a dreadful temper as a child and young woman. This led to frequent quarrels in the early years of her marriage 'but now my husband is always right'. Occasionally, she feels like 'exploding'. Then she retreats to her bedroom and tries to control the impulse to 'bash the place to bits'. She had difficulty in conceiving and did so only after some years. In the first few weeks of the baby's life she was sure he would die. She was unable to breast-feed. Lately she has suffered from excessive bleeding during menstruation. She feels all her troubles are sent by God to punish her.

This brief account gives us a picture of a woman whose everyday life is dominated by acute anxieties. Her attempt to control them by shutting herself in, and shutting the feared world out, in the hope of achieving peace is only partially successful. She is still left with her worry about her husband's safety and a feeling that her need to restrict her own life and that of her family makes her a bad wife and mother.

What we have learnt about Mrs B.'s phantasies so far is that the inside of her house is a place of relative peace and quiet, while the outside, the street, the world about which the newspapers bring reports, is a place of destruction and horror. The sharp juxtaposition of 'safe inside house' and 'dangerous outside world' is matched by her inner world which is either one of docility or one in which she smashes everything. So here we have concepts of security and danger, good and bad, passivity and aggression, right and wrong which have an either or, black-or-white quality about them with no shadings in between.

We might ask how did Mrs B. come to think of herself and the outside world in these terms? How has she in the course of her development come to conceive of safe places and dangerous spaces? What do house and street represent to her in phantasy? Why is anger felt to be completely destructive? What is the nature of the 'peace' she is seeking? Why does she conceive of something so punishing that it threatens her marriage, her creativity, her very existence?

Before attempting some answers, we will look briefly at what Mrs B. was able to tell the caseworker in the course of months of weekly visits, about her past. Mrs B. is the youngest of seven children. Her father died when she was six weeks old and she was subsequently cared for in the maternal aunt's home until her mother remarried. She was with her mother and step-father from the age of three until she was evacuated during the war at the age of seven. At first she was very unhappy, but later settled down and liked her foster-mother, though she remembers her as an anxious person. She did not wish to return home after the end of hostilities, and at her repeated request was allowed to stay on with the foster-parents for another two years, though her brothers and sisters went home. When she was eleven, step-father died. Two years after she had returned home the client's mother again remarried. Mrs B. remembers being so furious that she went to stay with her older sister who was then already married with two children. Four years later the sister's husband died. The client married at nineteen and as we know had difficulties in conceiving and feeding her baby. One-and-a-half years ago her mother-in-law collapsed in Mrs B.'s arms and subsequently died. Since then the client's symptoms have intensified.

We might say: given such experiences, little wonder that this woman is always expecting disaster! The client reported that a doctor told her that her troubles were due to all these deaths in the family, but what he said, had done nothing to alleviate her problems. Such an explanation is inadequate because it does not link the outer events to the person's inner experience in terms of phantasy. It became meaningful to her only when she was shown that she had attributed these deaths to herself and that they had been understood by her as a confirmation that her temper tantrums and jealousy were extremely dangerous, i.e. murderous. The client described herself as a head-strong, often bad-tempered child, and we know from her present-day feelings that 'temper' means something like destroying everything around her. It is significant that she has this feeling in the bedroom which must be associated with marriage and sexual relationships. Although we know little about her early life, she remembers being furious at her mother's third marriage, wanting to keep her to herself and feeling that the man was stealing mother from her. The extent of her anger with her mother is shown by her moving away from home, just as earlier she had insisted on staying with the foster-parents even when the war was over. She also recalled how angry she had been that her mother frequently left her at an earlier age in charge of older sisters while she went out to the pub. So we are presented with a division: a good 'house-mother' that the girl can possess—represented now by the good feelings while she is in the house—and the bad 'street-mother' associated with men, going out, leaving the girl, drinking—represented now by the street and its dangers.

Obviously the girl's anger did not kill off men and women in reality, though we have to assume that it did so in her phantasy. It is the omnipotence of thought and phantasy that leads to the fear and conviction that people have in fact been killed by anger. Actual deaths are taken as a confirmation that phantasy and mental phenomena are omnipotent. To the child, or the child inside the adult, it means: 'I need only think it, and it happens; my anger is so dangerous, the other one will die'. This feeling of being dangerous must have been strengthened in Mrs B.'s case by her being sent away from home twice, as if this was to say: Mother can only remarry, and a family survive, when you are not there. Indeed if we are to credit the client's story that the grandmother and step-father's deaths occurred during her periodic visits to the parental home, this would lend substance to her phantasy.

We can see in Mrs B. that such fears can lead to a severe control of aggression. She must always be docile and quiet and so must those around her. Her feeling that all aggression ends in disaster has led her to try and rid herself of it.

The more the destructive feelings are pushed out the more the outside (and others) come to be felt as a place filled with them. Not that there is any awareness that such projection has taken place—it is an *unconscious* phantasy 'action' of which only the result comes into consciousness: the world *is* bad and the house *is* good and peaceful. In this way the division between 'good inside house-mother' and 'bad outside-mother and men' has become strongly reinforced. Her own angry feelings with men are put into this outside world which is then felt to be killing to men. This explains her panic when her husband is late and her conviction that he must have been struck down.

The process is not completely successful and never can be: the internal war continues, feelings of exploding with anger and the fear of being sought out by a punishing killing God-father. But again we need to take note of the fact that Mrs B. is quite unaware *why* she feels herself to merit God's wrath. While she is out of touch with the source of her fear and guilt, namely her aggressiveness, there can be no change; for her very denial of aggressiveness—due to her fear of its omnipotent power —does not make it possible to bring it into the orbit of loving feelings which might modify and control it. There seems to be no concept in Mrs B. of a father who can act as a firm but kind policeman keeping her aggression under control. All the fathers Mrs B. knew died, and so must have appeared insufficiently strong to protect themselves and mother against destruction. The only powerful father is felt to be an extremely revengeful, punishing God.

The greatest help the caseworker can render this woman is to be aware of the client's reactions to herself; particularly when holidays or other occasions give rise to anger towards the worker and *her* husband, and to help her to verbalize, acknowledge and accept aggressive feelings. Any playing down of the client's hated feelings, in conflict with loving ones, would be taken as the worker's fear of them (like the husband who denies them) and so would serve to strengthen the client's conviction of their omnipotent power; conversely, their acceptance and the survival of the worker's marriage might lessen the belief in their omnipotence and so bring relief.

A case of school phobia

The above case strongly resembles a type of school phobia. While Mrs B. is afraid of open spaces, my patient Peter, aged fourteen, was afraid of entering buses and school and felt sick and dizzy when asked to do so. By the time I saw him he had stopped attending school altogether. Despite good intelligence, his school achievements had been poor. He was said to have kept apart from and been afraid of other boys. The parents were worried that he would not be able to get a job, as he could not go far away from home. Peter himself showed no urge to work. He demanded that mother be in the house, and serve his meals on time—he had never eaten school or restaurant meals—and he suggested that she had married the wrong man. When she went out, he wanted her to account for her every movement, to tell him whom she had spoken to and who kept her away so long. He watched carefully over the amount of food and affection that was given to his father and younger brother and compared it unfavourably to what he got. He sulked when visitors called, and if they had tea, complained that there would not be enough milk left for him.

His feelings of greed and ownership were evident from the beginning of treatment. The non-directive therapy session felt to him 'like walking into a strange house, helping yourself to the food in the larder and switching on the television'. He demanded more and more time, and more talking on my part, which was linked to his wish for more mental food experienced as mother's milk by a baby part of himself. He always came half-an-hour early and was watching out for me. In this way he was also helping himself to more than he was offered, looking into my life and my activities.

On one such occasion when he was sitting in the waiting-room long before he was due, he saw me talking to a male colleague and to another boy. When he came into my room he thought it was stuffy, musty-smelling, smoky like a bus and he did not think he could stay there. Then he got a stomach pain, rushed out and had an attack of diarrhoea. This sequence shows that when I did not fulfil his demand to be owned by him, enslaved as a larder-mother to provide for him alone, I became in his eyes filled with bad stuff; he turned away from me, not only externally but by turning me into sick food and getting rid of me via his anus.

This shows how he clings to his mother in a possessive way in order to avoid not only frustration but his hatred of a frustrating mother and the resulting attacks which turn her into a horrid and terrifying one. It makes it clear that the bus meant to him a mother who has men inside (the conductor and driver-father figures), and child passengers, while the school, as we came to see it, represented a mother full of rival children as well as master-fathers. In phantasy he attacks them, pushing into them his smells and wet! As a consequence, he experiences the inside of bus and school (which is felt by the baby part of him as a mother's body) to be a dirty, dangerous place full of counter-attacking children and men.

Infantile roots of persecutory anxieties

The infantile nature of the fears which we see in the

two cases indicates that they derive from an earlier stage of development. In children, a variety of phobias are indeed common and can usually be overcome with patience and tolerance. It is only when they persist, are extreme or seriously interfere with the child's life, that outside help may be necessary. In *Analysis of a Phobia in a Five-Year-Old Boy* (1909), Freud has given us a brilliant and delightful account of his first child case. Little Hans's phobic fears stemmed from his rivalry with his father for the love and possession of his mother and showed how sexual anxieties were transformed into a phobia of horses. Freud saw this as a symptom arising out of the Oedipal conflict, a conflict which he regarded as a part of normal emotional development in a five-year-old child. He saw also that he had been correct in claiming that elements of earlier development continue to exist in the depth of the mind and can be discovered in an adult's analysis.

Melanie Klein (1928) found fear of rivals and consequent anxieties to be equally common in still younger children. Furthermore, she saw the Oedipal genital desires of the boy and girl to have their forerunners in the baby's wish to own the feeding mother. We can see evidence of this earlier concept of father as a rival for mother's food in the fourteen-year-old Peter who watched carefully and resentfully over every morsel, particularly milk, given to father, brother and visitors. In Peter's case, the degree to which the possessiveness is still attached to the actual food and the extent to which it dominates over his more mature self, is extreme, but in small children such behaviour is common. Klein concluded that such feelings stemmed from early infancy; that whenever the infant is not being fed, he phantasies that mother is giving her breast to a rival: to father, brother or even herself.

Such 'baby-feelings' in relation to a person who is felt to be able to provide physical or mental food, security and love continue to exist to some extent throughout life; they are particularly active in any emotionally dependent relationship and particularly pressing in times of stress and crisis. The client may thus have strong feelings about the caseworker. Whenever she is not attending to him he is likely to experience her as putting her husband, children and other clients before him or withholding treatment for her own benefit. To the extent that such feelings are operative, he perceives the caseworker—as the infant the mother—in terms of his own needs; we might say: in a self-centred way.

Focusing attention on the motivation underlying behaviour, Klein found that this attitude of: 'I need you, I must have you all the time', is based not only on greed and possessiveness, but is a way of keeping at bay terrible anxieties such as 'I am so frightened when you, the good and helpful one, go away': 'I cannot survive without your presence': 'I'll die'.

It would be rare for a child or adult to put this directly into words. A child might cling or scream in desperation and the intense cry of the baby conveys the message of 'I'm dying', 'I'm in danger' so forcefully, it compels us to rush to his aid. With adolescents and adults, we may have to be more perceptive to understand their cries for help; it may be delinquent or criminal behaviour, done so openly that it shows an unconscious wish to be found out; it may be accident-proneness; or just a feeling that is conveyed which makes us worried and concerned about the safety of our client. In every case we have to decide how far this is based on the client's anxiety and to what extent it is used to manipulate and control us.

As Klein has shown (1963), it is not simply a fear of being left alone but left *with* something: with terror. The content of the terror may be manifold: the fear of exposure to one's self-hatred and suicidal impulses; of hatred of the other person and fear of retaliation; of robbers and plotters; of witches and ghosts; of utter physical or mental helplessness; fear of the unknown, which is always felt to be potentially dangerous. While the content varies from one person to the other, the common factor is the fear of death or harm that might befall one in the absence of the good and helpful other person.

Klein distinguished between these *fears centred round the safety of the self*: persecutory or paranoid anxieties and what she called *depressive anxieties: fears centred round the safety of others* (1934 and 1946).

Klein related these fears of a bad 'presence' in the absence of the good mother to the projection of hate, and following from this, an expectation of a hating, death- or harm-inflicting outside force. We saw in the case of Mrs B. how her attempt to rid herself of aggression led to her pushing it out and so constantly increasing her fear of a bad external world. We saw in Peter, how this jealousy of rivals and his phantasied attacks on them, turned me in his mind into both an external dangerous person and internally into a frightening object. The fear of this bad frightening 'other' in turn increased his greed for the presence of the good mother to act as a barrier against hatred and the experience of a 'bad' one.

These feelings may sound so irrational as to appear mad. Why, we could argue, did Peter, who after all could see and hear me and who had previously experienced me as helpful, not tell himself that I was the same person as the one he now found so frightening? Indeed, by inter- preting to him and recognizing that a baby part of him felt terrified and was temporarily ruling over the more adult part of him that knew me as a helping therapist, I enabled him to return to my room. In making this distinction, I was not attempting to reassure him but rather inviting the more mature part of him to look with me at an infantile part of himself: to study this infant inside him who concretely experienced me as forcing back into him the smoke and dirt with which I was felt to be filled. It makes sense when these feelings are seen to be rooted in infancy, at a time when there is no or little recognition that the mother who has been hated and attacked in her absence and turned into a frightening one is the same as the one who feeds and loves him. The baby cannot distinguish between internal and external experiences so that whatever his phantasies, they are thought to have concrete effects on the external mother as well as her representation in his mind and body. Also the young infant has, as far as we know, no concept of time or of the existence of an object in time and this lends to the experience a quality of 'now or never', all or none, either all good or all bad. There is no tomorrow, no sometimes good and sometimes bad, some food now and some later.

Defences against persecutory anxieties

Out of persecutory fears: of starvation, death and a hostile force, arises the need for something or somebody strong enough to deal with them. Hence a phantasy of an all-powerful ever-present good mother. She is not good in an ordinary sense, she is idealized: her body and mind are thought to contain endless ·supplies of food, warmth, strength, knowledge. To be with her means never to want, never to feel helpless, never to be frightened. It follows that this idealized object has no needs of its own; it is god-like, above all human frailty and failure, sufficient unto itself; selfish and mean if it does not give unendingly of its bounty. Just as the infant feels empty, so mother's breast is felt to be full and in his wish to possess this full object and be safe against all fears that assail him, he may wish not only to be fed but to get right inside, to burrow into this treasure-house, rob it and make off with it, or possess it with a 'king of the castle' feeling of ownership and control, like the little boy who said to me: 'You are Great Britain and I rule over you'. Or he may wish to dwell inside mother's body like a parasite (a 'kept' man) on her riches, or he may put himself inside her in phantasy (projective identification; compare Klein

1955) and his image of himself become so fused with her that he feels himself to acquire the qualities of the idealized mother and have illusions of grandeur.

The more helpless, the more threatened by persecutory anxieties the infant (or infant part of the adult), the more desperate are the measures he uses to defend himself against such anxieties. The feelings about mother's inside or part of her body, as either full of riches, life, love or at other times under dominance of hostile feelings full of evil enemies, biting, robbing, etc., are later transferred to other places. We saw how Mrs B. felt the inside of her house to be like a mother: gentle, orderly and peaceful, while the outside was like the disorderly, drunk, murderous mother with men. Peter clung to mother and her house as the good one, while the school and bus represented a mother already possessed by men and children wishing to kill, poison and suffocate him. Klein discovered that learning inhibitions were often related to the fear of finding out; to the infantile part of the child that means going into mother's body with all the anxieties and dangers lurking inside her.

Klein stated (1946) that such splitting, i.e. the very definite division of mother into a good and bad one is an essential stage in the emotional development of the young infant. It enables him to sort his experiences, bring order into chaos by separating out and keeping relatively safe all those parts of himself and those of mother which promote life and growth from those forces inside and outside him that threaten life and safety. Such trust in an ideal object is necessary for the small infant (and D. W. Winnicott, 1964, states that the mother must at first fit in with this omnipotent phantasy of the baby) to enable him to sustain hope and thus make otherwise intolerable anxiety of his annihilation bearable. Loving feelings attach themselves to the mother who provides satisfaction and relief and at first the infant tends to feel that this good mother *is* himself. Hating feelings tend to attach themselves to the mother who is felt to be responsible for frustrations and pain. The wish to dissociate himself from this bad object, on to whom he also projects his own destructiveness, leads to the need for and so promotes recognition of someone other than self, of separateness, of me and not me, inside me and outside.

While persecutory anxieties and the defences against them which we discussed above are seen as part of normal development, they provide no permanent solution. For instance, the idealized object, the moment it fails to live up to the ideal expectations put upon it, quickly turns into its opposite. The perfect mother always available when needed, turns at a flash into a purposefully starving, withholding, inflicting suffering one; in other words, she becomes the persecutory mother whom the belief in an ideal one was meant to keep at bay. We may link this to our observation that babies change so abruptly from a state of utter bliss to one of total raging despair. We see it too in those adults who experience the world in terms of black and white, finding people and things at one moment heavenly, at the next horrid. Idealization cannot work ultimately, because no human being can fulfil the demand to be 'ideal'. An intolerance of the pain of disillusionment may lead to holding on to the belief that an ideal exists somewhere and result in constant changes of job, partners, friends, domicile, in the hope of eventually finding one that will satisfy the ideal requirements. The search is bound to be fruitless and end in failure. Such failure to come to grips with reality and its limitations (and basically one's own) precludes finding a solution to a problem, making use of one's own abilities to set about coming to grips with a problem, for the other person is expected to provide the answer. Ultimately it leads to poor judgment, to flatness of feeling and a lack of knowledge of others and oneself. For all this is an attempt to get rid of, or blur over destructive feelings in the individual himself, and so he is cut off both from understanding himself and others with their dual nature perpetually in conflict and producing a spectrum of different shades of feelings.

The different defensive measures which have been described, regarded as normal in the infant, may also be so in the adult if employed temporarily in periods of stress. They become pathological only if extreme and/or maintained permanently. We saw an example of this in the 'frightened client' at the beginning of this chapter, who increasingly turned away from a bad external world, (constantly deteriorating because of her evacuation into it of her own destructive feelings) and clinging to a precariously maintained but highly idealized inner world. In other cases such a process could lead to living in a world of phantasy and illusions of grandeur mixed with feelings of paranoia. It is the *extent* of the *splitting*, the inability to tolerate aggression internally, and the *massive projection* which make it pathological.

To some extent we all have a tendency to idealize. This enters, for instance, into falling in love, while on the other hand a need to continue to idealize the partner at all costs, would bar the way to a real love-relationship based on being able to accept at least some of the faults of the other person. Idealization also helps us in adversity to maintain hope for a brighter future; on the other hand, a lack of appreciation of the difficulties to be overcome, makes us aim for unrealistic goals and set about achieving these in an omnipotent way which precludes their attainment. Splitting makes it possible to maintain one kind of attitude and feeling at a time, leaving whatever contradicts it out of our conscious mind, and projecting it into someone else. This process can often be observed in work with groups, when each faction expels feelings which to some extent are held by the whole group. This tendency to keep opposing emotions separated, whether in different people or split off from one another in one's own mind, comes from the wish to avoid inner conflict.

PERSECUTORY ANXIETIES AND DEFENCES AGAINST THEM

An understanding of persecutory anxieties and their defences can help us in diagnosis. We may ask ourselves to what extent is the client predominantly under the sway of such primitive anxieties or defences against them and how much do they influence the way in which he relates to his environment. It is a clue to his emotional immaturity if he is primarily doing so in terms of the anxieties and defensive attitudes here described.

2

Depressive anxieties and defences against them in adult, child and infant

What is meant by 'Depression'?

'Depression' is an umbrella term which we use to cover a variety of painful emotional states. It may refer to a passing mood of 'being down in the dumps', or a more or less permanent state of misery. The miserable feelings may appear without apparent cause or arise in a particular situation. A simple example would be a boy tearing up the picture he has just painted, complaining: 'It's all a mess'; or a little girl sitting in a corner crying: 'Mummy's gone away and she will never come back', although told that Mummy will return in a quarter of an hour.

A client might say: 'What's the use of telling you my troubles, nobody can understand or help me anyway'. In this instance, it is the worker who is made to feel despairing and useless. We might be dealing with recurrent periods of depression in which the client feels unable to work and decide anything, or with dissipated feelings of pessimism, sometimes alternating with periods of frivolity and over-confidence. In its more extreme form, depression is associated with suicide on the one hand and a slowing down of physical and mental functions on the other.

What is common to all these painful states, though in

varying degrees of severity and permanence, is the lack of belief in something good, either in oneself or in others. Such misery is associated with hopelessness. We might ask ourselves, how does this come about? What attacks the hope? Let us look at an example with a view to studying the nature of depressive feelings.

A distressed client

The Child Care Officer went to see Mrs O. to consider her request to have her nine-months-old baby daughter placed for adoption. She found this mother to be an apparently warm-hearted person, able to run a home comfortably. She spoke with a good deal of affection about her husband and the other two children. She talked easily and cried frequently in the course of the interviews which revealed the following story:

In the early days of the marriage, there had been acute financial hardship and the birth of their eldest child, now aged nine, added to the burden. Gradually Mr O.'s position improved, and when they were financially reasonably secure the couple had another little girl. Once the children were at school, Mrs O. helped the family finances by going out to work, thus relieving her husband from doing over-time. His health had begun to give cause for some concern, though he was not actually ill.

Then Mrs O. was dismayed to find herself once more pregnant. She had not planned to have more children, and a new baby meant that she would no longer be able to go out to work. Slowly she became reconciled to the idea of another child, believing that 'after all, it would be nice to have a boy'. She even began looking forward to the event. One month before her confinement, Mrs O. was told that she was having twins. She was acutely shocked, refused to accept this and continued to refer to carrying one baby.

When the twins were born, the stronger one was a boy

and he remained in the cot next to his mother, she was able to feed him and find pleasure in tending to him. The other twin was a little girl, underweight and weak. She was immediately removed to a Premature Baby Unit, where at first she had to be kept in an incubator. Mrs O. never saw this little girl during her stay in hospital and when she was discharged was about to leave the ward with the baby boy when a surprised nurse stopped her and said, 'Aren't you going to see your daughter?' Mrs O. said that she felt dazed. She allowed herself to be led to the cot, but was quite unable to make a move towards her baby, whereupon the nurse put the little girl firmly into mother's arms. Mrs O. said: 'At that moment I felt faint'. She could barely stand and does not know how she did not drop the baby.

Subsequently, she refused to collect the little girl from the hospital and did so only after weeks of persuasion. Mrs O. reported with some bitterness how a doctor had told her to pull herself together and that as an experienced mother she ought to love this child as she did the others. She said that she needed no telling as to how she *ought* to feel. She knew that perfectly well, but could not herself understand why the feeling of love she had for her other children could not be extended to this child.

Eventually when the little girl was six weeks old, Mr and Mrs O. took the baby home. Mrs O. described how she fed, bathed and clothed her as rapidly as possible with light finger movements, trying not to touch her and her clothes and food more than was absolutely essential. She did not tie ribons on her frocks, she put the pram covers on carefully and left this baby as quickly and as frequently as she could with a neighbour or her husband while she went out with the twin-boy. There were no indications that the little girl was other than an easy baby to manage: no stories of crying or refusing food. Mrs O. described with great feeling how sometimes at night she would get on her knees by the baby's cot, crying and praying that she would be given love for this baby, but it never worked.

Throughout this time her husband had been patient and helped as much as possible in the care of the mother and babies. He had resisted her request to have the little girl adopted, but by now he could no longer stand his wife's distress and felt that for her sake and the other children's, adoption might after all be the only solution. He was sure that his wife genuinely felt that this baby also should have the opportunity to be loved.

What makes this story so moving is that we feel ourselves taken right into this woman's inner struggle. It is worth noting that the sensitive listener reacts differently to a depressed person than to a paranoid one. While the fears and emotions which the latter experiences may alarm us or evoke pity and concern about the hell he lives in, the depressed person makes us aware of the tragedy in which he is involved. We sense in him a potential for love though the person suffering from depression, like Mrs O., complains of an *inability to love*. Mrs O. appears able to love her other children. We note also that she is able to feel concern for her husband's health, and indeed this worry was one reason why she did not wish to have more children. After the initial dismay about her pregnancy she was able to come to terms with it and make a loving relationship with the twin-boy. Nor do we get the impression that the relationship to the twin-girl is one of undiluted hatred—rather that Mrs O. is terrified that her hostility will result in injury of the baby. She clearly feels that she might drop, poison or suffocate the baby, and to prevent this she makes herself touch and handle her lightly, tie no ribbons, and save the baby by handing it over to others. Her love stops her from actively harming the baby, her hatred from loving it. This is the impasse in which she finds herself.

Definition of depressive anxiety

If we compare Mrs O. to Mrs B. (in the previous chapter) one difference at once becomes obvious. While Mrs B. worries primarily about her own safety, Mrs O. is primarily worried about what her hate will do to the baby. Mrs B. is afraid of the terrible outside world which contains destruction while she and her home are 'safe and good'; Mrs O. is aware of her own destructiveness, the dangers arising from within her. This then is the difference: the paranoid person projects aggression, the depressed person has taken back into himself some of his innate destructiveness, and fears the consequences it has had or will have on those dear to him. We see, therefore, that *depressive anxiety arises out of the conflict of ambivalence— the love and hate experienced towards one and the same person.*

We are now in a position to answer our earlier question about what attacks the hope? The depressed person has lost his belief in the strength of his loving capacity, feels that his destructiveness is more powerful than his love and that therefore he will fail, or has already failed, to protect the person he cares for. But how has such a state of affairs come about? It is in complete contrast to the feeling of idealization of goodness described in the previous chapter.

Roots of depressive anxieties in childhood and infancy

When we looked at the individual's growing relationship to another, originally that of the child to his mother, we stated that the world was at first experienced in terms of black and white, wonderful and terrible; the idealized mother who represents life, security and hope, and on the other hand, the wicked one who inflicts pain and suffering and threatens life. We followed the child, clinging to an external idealized partner and by taking in this ideal relationship establishing an ideal mother inside who is to protect him against harm.

What then has happened in the mental structure of the person who sees no white, no goodness, but only dreary grey left in the world and himself, that befogs the outlook into the future? We do not gain the impression from Mrs O. that black and white, good and bad have become confused. Rather that love and hate confront each other like two opposing forces, interlocked and blocking each other. In this impasse the person may either feel immobilized or he may resort to desperate action.

Let us look at the developing relationship of the baby to his mother. In Klein's view, (1948), something like the following happens:—on the basis of repeated experiences of a mother who can cope with and contain his destructiveness and fear, the baby gains confidence in the strength of the good mother. He establishes this inside himself, i.e. in phantasy, he takes in or introjects a strong mother. As he becomes less frightened of aggression, the need to project it lessens and he can begin to contain some of his destructiveness. Because he is less persecuted, he needs to idealize mother less and she can gradually be seen as ordinarily good. His concepts of ideally wonderful and frighteningly terrible become less extreme and are replaced by good and bad, both in terms of his mother and himself. But the good and bad feelings are still felt to be directed towards two separate people. He loves the good mother who feeds and comforts him; he hates the bad mother who frustrates and hurts him.

There comes a time when the infant realizes that the mother he loves and the one he attacks in rage, anger and jealousy are different aspects of one and the same person. At this point he is faced with the dilemma that he hates and attacks the very person on whom he depends for life and love. Moreover, while an ideal mother was felt to be beyond the realm of harm, a merely good mother has human qualities of frailty. Such realizations bring with them intense emotional pain for he fears that his hatred in reality and phantasy has already done or will do damage, or destroy the good mother; and that his greedy demands have depleted her strength and supplies. Klein called such *anxiety for the safety and well-being of the loved person: depressive anxiety*.

The child may at that stage need his mother's presence to reassure him that she is in fact all right, for in her absence he fears that she is ill, dead and lost to him, as she is in his phantasy. Her safe reappearance as a person who cares, a breast that can still feed, hands that can still remove his messes, eyes giving him her attention and love, are essential to reassure the infant that his destructiveness has not resulted in injury or death. Thus, he learns to distinguish between the internally attacked and damaged mother and the external more resilient mother, between phantasy/internal reality, on the one hand, and external reality, on the other.

Depressive anxieties become particularly acute during weaning. The baby may feel that the mother stops feeding him because he has emptied the breast or that she takes it away because he is too dangerous. Similarly, clients capable of depressive anxiety will be worried that they are overburdening the caseworker with their anxiety and needs, making too heavy demands on her, wearing her out. Should she leave her job they will fear that they have exhausted her, overloaded her or by their doubts and attacks undermined her belief in her ability to help them.

Depressive feelings in turn bring in their wake guilt, grief and sadness. If these can be borne, they lead eventually to the wish to spare the loved one and make good the damage already done. Out of the desire to spare mother, babies start to wait for their feeds, even sometimes to wean themselves. Children learn to control their sphincters and let mother go in spite of powerful worry. Clients learn to contain their troubles until the time of their appointment and to respect the limits of the case-worker's function. But in spite of the attempt to spare and to control anger and jealousy, destructive feelings will continue to exist; even if they are controlled during daytime, they recur in sleep.

Out of the feelings of sadness that the loved person is attacked again and again, there arises the wish to make good the damage done internally and externally. Such reparation may take many forms: e.g. the baby may stroke the mother's breast, smile at her and wish to feed her. An older child may want to help mother, or engage in constructive play. The school child will begin to work harder, and the adult restores by all sorts of kindly thoughts and acts, as well as in constructive work and creative art. For the wish to be reparative stimulates the development of skills and interests.

Such development does not occur in a straight progression. Feelings of depression are extremely painful, for they involve doubt about the survival of love in the face of hatred. The pain and doubts about one's goodness lead easily to despair: the despair that one is incapable of protecting or restoring the loved person. To evade the pain of guilt, the child and adult tries to deny that he is destructive. He may claim that he is 'not like that'. That is to say, he again deals with the bad part of himself by splitting it off either from conscious awareness or on to someone else. We can detect in this a feeling of being held responsible, and indeed when the person feels accused he looks for someone else to attack and blame, such as 'It's all these coloured immigrants', 'It's the school's fault', etc. Alternatively, the harm done may be denied. 'What does it matter?' said a child who broke a window, 'I couldn't care less'. Or the value of the particular person may be denied, like the boy who, immediately after his beloved father's death, remarked cheerfully 'When will we get another Daddy?' Such attitudes, i.e. the denial of the uniqueness of a particular relationship, the denial of responsibility, the denial of harm done, are called 'manic defences', because they are an escape into gaiety or 'care-less-ness' away from the depressive feelings which are felt to be unendurable. If this becomes a permanent state, absence of care and concern leads to callousness, some-times to psychopathic behaviour in which the value of the other person's life, property and feelings are denied.

Quite a different attitude was shown by Mrs O. There we saw a woman who was concerned and struggling against her hate, yet unable to achieve a good relationship with her baby. In this and the following cases we shall look at some of the factors that may hinder the working-out of the depressive conflict.

Different kinds of depressive anxiety:
inability to bear depressive pain: depressive illness

The rejected twin
Why did Mrs O. fail in her attempt to find love for the baby? The answer is no doubt complicated and we only know some of the factors in this case. We know that she felt a new pregnancy threatened her ability to work and so her husband's health. Thus, from the beginning, the new baby was felt to be unwanted, and to some extent, a bad, spoiling baby, who added to her worries.

She dealt with her ambivalence by deciding to love a particular baby, a baby boy, possibly because she saw in him a potential source of support for her husband and the family. When she learnt that she was having twins, her ambivalence turned to denial of a second baby, that is to say, in her mind, in phantasy it was annihilated. Fate played into her phantasy in that she had a boy and a girl, and her feelings of a bad, unwanted baby were now com-pletely split off on to the girl. Moreover, the girl's weak-ness made her feel that her thoughts of wanting to kill her had affected the baby's size and health. The fact that she did not have the opportunity of seeing the baby at first must have added to her suspicion that the baby had in fact died. When given the chance to see her, she was almost unable to look into the baby's face. To this mother it meant facing a baby towards whom she had harboured murderous thoughts and in consequence felt extremely guilty. We might speculate that it was her feeling of guilt towards a helpless and weak baby and her doubts about being able to restore it, that hindered her ability to love it. However, we cannot say this with any conviction until we know more about this mother. I shall draw on the experience of a similar case which I treated, in the hope that it will throw light on the kind of anxieties involved.

Mrs P. was the young mother of twin-girls. Both twins were underweight at birth but the elder girl, Pamela, was heavier and stronger by far than her little sister, Pauline, who only weighed three pounds. Both babies needed three-hourly feeds, but Pauline was at first unable to suck and had to be fed drop by drop with a pipette. Mother was extremely doubtful about her ability to love Pauline. She was beside herself when she cried and could not pacify the baby; but it was almost worse when the baby made no sound for any length of time. The mother would rush to the cot and listen for her breathing, terrified that the baby might die. In talking about the twins she always called Pamela by name, but referred to Pauline as 'it' or 'the other twin'. This could be seen as her inability to feel the twin-girl to be a person, an alive child. It was as if she were trying to protect herself against the pain of the baby's anticipated death by not investing hope and love in her in the first place.

In the course of treatment, I found myself put into two different roles by the mother. Sometimes I was seen as capable, firm and understanding; at other times, particularly at the beginning of interviews or after a holiday, or if she could detect any traces of tiredness in me, I was seen as a weak person who must not be burdened with her troubles. She was in some ways an exhausting patient, for often she made me work hard by withholding relevant information so that I felt I had to do all the work, even that part of it of which she was capable. At other times, and particularly at the end of interviews, she would swamp me with so much that I was hard put to absorb and interpret some of what she told me and contain the rest until the next time. She had difficulty in getting started at the beginning of the interview and found it hard to stop at the end of it. Sometimes I was tempted to run over the time because the patient conveyed the impression that she could not be abandoned when the work was not completed. All this was interpreted to her in terms of my being a therapist (mother) into whose mind (breast) she emptied her problems, her unwanted messes at the end of the hour, so that they could be left with me; that then she could not talk to me at the beginning of the next hour because she experienced me as a worn-out mother; worn out because I had been asked to carry so much for the patient in the interim, and literally occupied by her so that she feared I would have no chance to recover during the break. Indeed, quite often, having been given a complex dream by this patient right at the end of the hour, I would find it difficult to free my mind for other people and other things.

When I had to miss a few sessions because of an attack of influenza, Mrs P. found it difficult to resume treatment. She said that perhaps after all it did not help her. Anyway she was so busy with the babies and the financial expense was great. Previous work with her convinced me that she was afraid that *she* was not worth *my* effort, because in spite of my help she felt she had not improved enough. Furthermore, my illness had reinforced her fear that I was exhausted and over-burdened by her. When these anxieties were interpreted, she cried and experienced great relief, and her positive feelings for the analytic work returned stronger than before. (My patient had in the meantime asked her mother about her early history and learned that her mother had often felt tired and depressed during the early months of my patient's life; the mother had in fact been advised to go away to have a rest, but she had stayed with the baby.)

Soon after my illness the patient reported the following dream:—There were two pear trees laden with fruit and she stood contemplating their beauty and thinking how appetizing they looked. She rushed forward eagerly to pick and bite into a pear, but as she did so, it changed into a shrivelled-up thing as did the rest of the fruit on that tree. The pears on the other tree were also affected but not to the same extent. Next, she saw two little girls dancing in front of the trees, one looked thin, pale and poorly, while the other was round and had a healthy complexion. In this revealing dream Mrs P. shows the two ways in which she conceives of me and her mother: as the full, beautiful mother-breast and the damaged, shrivelled one. It also gives us an explanation of how the change from one to the other occurs. It is the stormy, greedy way in which she rushes and bites into the desired fruit (breast) that makes it thin and shrivelled. (In the transference to me, her reticence at the beginning of interviews was a defence against storming into me, and reducing me to a shrunken object.) This feeling is kept to one pear tree, one breast. We may assume that as a baby it was the first breast offered which was taken by storm, while once the hunger was appeased the second breast could be approached in a gentler mood and so was felt to suffer less and retain more of its soundness.

What is also clarified in this dream is the link between the breasts and the two little girls—that is to say, her twin daughters, who were experienced by part of her as if they were her mother's breasts, one weakly and damaged and the other strong. The weakly one was felt to be so severely damaged that Mrs P. doubted her capacity to keep the baby alive. The exhaustion and depression of her mother when Mrs P. was a baby must have strengthened her fear that her greed was so great that no-one was strong enough to withstand depletion. Once Mrs P. had gained insight into these aspects of the relationship, her feeling for Pauline changed dramatically. She could now distinguish between her baby-relationship to her own mother and her more adult abilities to be a mother to her own baby; and so she was able to love the baby with particular tenderness.

It may sound strange that a baby could evoke feelings that related to Mrs P.'s relationship to her own mother. If, however, we allow for the fact that every experience is stored in the mind, it becomes less strange that the earliest experiences in life and all aspects of that relationship enter into later ones which bear some similarity to the original one. Klein stated (1935) that where the depressive anxieties in this first relationship have not been dealt with successfully, the individual will be predisposed to depressive illness in later life.

A battered baby

Mrs R.'s six-months-old baby had to be admitted to hospital after severe bruising. It is significant that she herself brought the baby for attention, but at first denied responsibility for the injury. When seen by a psychiatrist in the presence of a Child Care Officer the mother appeared very controlled and tense. Her expression was mask-like and devoid of feeling. The baby was subsequently fostered, though after one year it was considered safe for him to return home. Meanwhile the Child Care Officer had worked with mother at weekly intervals.

The baby was reported to have cried incessantly from birth. Sometimes he could be comforted by being carried around on mother's shoulder but often she found nothing that would stop his cries. Mother said eventually she had sometimes gone out in order not to hear him screaming— 'It cut into me like a saw and I felt he was constantly complaining that nothing I did for him was any good'. When put to the breast, he would turn away from it or else suck hungrily and then sick up much of it. 'It made me feel that I was feeding him poison', Mrs R. said. She had so much wanted a boy, because it would please her mother and to some extent help to make up for the latter's loss of her own infant boy. She had wanted her mother to help her bring up the baby and was angry that the Housing Authorities had not arranged for her to have a flat near her.

Here we catch a glimpse of this baby being something of a gift to Mrs R.'s mother. Mrs R. remembered being jealous when her younger brother was born and feeling guilty at his death and hence wished to make amends to her mother by sharing her own baby boy. But her baby's difficulties made her doubt her goodness and he acted as an accuser, someone who mocked her—'You only make baby boys be sick and distressed, your breasts are no good. They are little girl ones, you have nothing to offer but faeces and urine.' So from feeling depressed and concerned about the baby and her own mother, his apparent rejection of her made her kindly feelings gradually change into unbearable despair and eventually hatred. At first she attempted to run away from this 'persecutor' and eventually she tried to silence his accusing voice by knocking the baby against the wall and thus nearly killing him.

This example shows how depressive feelings of being not good enough are strengthened by experiences which seem to confirm this. We all tend to hate, try to avoid, run away from, or in turn, criticize those who criticize us. Their accusing voice finds an echo inside ourselves where our own doubts about our worthiness, goodness and ability to be constructive lie more or less near the surface. It is, therefore, instructive to consider how we behave when someone questions or disapproves of our actions, or our behaviour or views. The vehemence with which we tend to defend ourselves may be an indication of underlying uncertainty. Alternatively, we may avoid our critic or in turn put him into the situation of being in the wrong, so as to evade the awareness that there may be a grain of truth in what he says. Mostly, we tend to seek the company of those who reassure us and make us feel good and important.

In the close family relationships it becomes almost impossible to run away and avoid emotional conflicts, and it is here that the most intense drama of love and hate, wishing to kill and wishing to make good again, are lived out.

An abandoned baby
The Probation Officer visited Mrs Q. in prison. She had left her third child, aged fourteen months, in a railway-station waiting-room, hoping that someone would take her little girl home and care for it. She felt this child to be different from her other children. She could not satisfy her, 'The baby refused food, screamed, sat with clenched fists, often used to bite me and I could not stand the smell of her faeces'. Mrs Q.'s other children are boys and she herself was the only girl in her parents' family. She remembers intense, fierce competition with her older brothers and thought they were much preferred by both parents. At the age of five she was boarded out with maternal grandmother because her elder brother, as well as her mother, had contracted tuberculosis.

In the course of the interviews Mrs Q. showed that she had experienced being sent away as a way of their protecting themselves against her biting and dirtying and that she had felt responsible for her mother's and brother's illness. She had been worried about other people's health as long as she could remember and expected her mother to die from year to year. Abandoning her daughter could thus be seen as Mrs Q.'s attempt to get rid of the poisonous, biting part of herself which she had not thought about again since her childhood until she had a 'biting, smelling' daughter. She felt this 'girl-part' to be so dangerous to the rest of the family that it had to be pushed out of the family circle. We can see here that the baby is in the mother's mind confused with the baby-part of herself, a part which causes depressive anxiety if taken into the family, or rather into Mrs Q.'s inner self, and is instead expelled as too bad and causing too much worry to be admitted.

Thus a bad part of the self may be split off in order to save the 'good' mother and her family.

A problem family

The Y. family were living in the basement of a condemned house. Although four rooms were available, the seven members of the family virtually lived in only one. A dim light was burning there while the rest of the flat was in utter darkness. The bedding was filthy and inadequate, the floor strewn with remains of food, ashes and bits of paper. Father worked intermittently; he continued to stay in bed for long periods after a bout of illness and also took to his bed whenever he changed his place of work. Mother looked under-nourished and worn out and sometimes could not make the effort to cook for the family. In spite of this, she insisted on the children coming home at midday. The eldest boy had been before the Courts, having been caught as a member of a gang engaged in pilfering.

It is the kind of family dealt with, at one and the same time, by a number of social agencies, yet one which fails to benefit from all the services offered. The despair and sense of failure they induce in those social workers involved with them is in itself an indication of what the family projects: that it is futile even to attempt to 'get their house in order', or rather the family's affairs and their internal world. They appear to have almost given up the struggle and instead given themselves over to despair and apathy. But in so doing, the mess accumulates and in consequence the problems become ever more difficult to tackle. Thus, Mr Y.'s repeated failure to resume work left the family finances in even greater ruins. When Mrs Y. did not clean the flat, the rubbish piled up and in consequence she felt more despondent.

Moreover, their behaviour evoked disapproval and threats from a number of Authorities; this in return made them feel that they were unfairly treated and regarded as bad, negligent parents. For instance, when their son Joe required a hearing aid and mother was asked to take him to hospital to see a specialist, she repeatedly failed to keep the appointments. She told the family caseworker that she went to the bus stop but as the bus did not come for fifteen minutes she set off home again. Anyway, what would the specialist say : that she did not feed him right? After several missed appointments, Mrs Y. received a threatening letter from the school authorities and this made her feel criticized, accused and that people in authority were always against her.

It was at this point that the family caseworker began visiting the family. He was greeted with great suspicion as yet another person claiming the right to intrude. He listened to the expressions of hostility without being frightened by them, nor needing to assure mother of his friendly feelings. He simply said that he appreciated how she felt but that it was his duty to see that Joe's hearing was attended to. What he would like to talk to her about was *why* she felt she could not take the child to the hospital. In this way he established himself from the outset as a parent who, while taking the client's *feelings* into consideration, yet out of concern for their welfare, controls and *set limits* to *actions* taken or left undone. He showed that he respected the family's privacy by fixing the times at which he would call. He also said that he would visit regularly over the next nine months, demonstrating thereby that he considered them a worthwhile investment of his time and that he would not give up easily. This seemed almost at once to produce a feeling of hopefulness in both Mr and Mrs Y.

In the course of the contact with the Y. parents, the caseworker learnt that offers of material assistance and advice were not only not taken up by them, but produced feelings of resentment and depression. This could be seen as arising from feeling belittled, like children when they are helped in situations where they can with some encouragement do things themselves. Instead, the caseworker learnt to help them in their efforts to help themselves. Again, one can draw a parallel to an adolescent who wishes to be independent, hates interference but at times needs a parent's presence or active assistance to be able to cope with a difficult situation. For instance, not only did the caseworker explore the reasons why Mrs Y. felt she could not take the child to hospital, he also accompanied her on their visit to the specialist. Thus, he acted as a parent, helping Mrs Y. and her son to live through this anxious experience. He also assisted Mr Y. in the painting of the flat and showed him how he could improve the plumbing; but it was Mr Y. who set about finding himself a better job.

Within a few months a new atmosphere prevailed. The home was cleaned up, more rooms used and lit. Mother could now allow the children to stay for school lunches and this enabled them to make relationships outside the family. It appeared that mother had previously kept her flock around her because she could only feel alive as long as she was constantly needed by them. And independence on her children's part meant to her that she was rejected, unwanted, unloved. It would seem that this revived earlier feelings, for after nine months of apparently good mothering, Mrs Y. had lost her mother and been with a number of foster families. Mr Y. came from a home where discipline was inconsistent; sometimes his father would beat him and at other times he indulged him. His conflict with his father, obedience and revolt against discipline, were repeated in his inconsistent work pattern.

If we look for the primary factor which brought about such dramatic improvement in the Y. family, it would seem to lie in the steady relationship of a caring case-worker. Such a relationship implies, in the first instance, the need for someone to care and accept hostile and despairing feelings. Another essential element in it is the setting of limits to the invasion of sloth and negligence, as also to more actively destructive and self-destructive action. Such firm caring brings help and support to the constructive and reparative drives; indeed, this family, like other similar ones, found untapped resources within themselves. The experience of success in turn helps to alleviate despair and strengthen the belief in the capacity to overcome difficulties.

Problem families attract attention because they have become a burden to society, but the basic attitudes they show are not unusual. There is in everyone a tendency to waste time, opportunity and talent and just drift along, to abandon himself to feelings that it is not worth his while to make the effort or that parents and society owe him an easier existence. 'Letting things go' in turn intensifies the feelings of depression and hopelessness. The capacity to be reparative is deficient in most of us.

Some factors contributing to the difficulty in dealing with depressive anxieties

We have looked at a number of cases in which individuals were unable to tolerate depressive anxieties and the result was a depressive illness. I would like to pick out some of the external and internal factors which can contribute to depression.

External factors:
Early experience of loss. Mrs Y., the mother in the problem family discussed, had lost her mother at an early age and never overcome the feelings of rejection and persecution connected with this event. A mother who in fact deserts the baby undermines the baby's belief in the existence of a good caring mother and strengthens the feeling of possessing a persecuting bad mother. It also encourages the feeling that one's destructiveness is omnipotent and that one can do nothing to bring the good mother back.

A very vulnerable mother. Mrs P., mother of the weak twin and Mrs Q. whose mother contracted TB, both had to deal in early childhood with mothers who were either depressed or ill. Such an experience would reinforce in the baby/child feelings of being very damaging and exhausting. It may also lead to hopelessness about being able to make others happy and well. Thus we saw that Mrs P., faced with a delicate baby, withdrew her loving feelings and felt unable to keep it alive, while Mrs Q. tried to get rid of the bad 'baby-part' of herself in abandoning her baby.

Internal factors:
Inability to tolerate pain. It would seem that the ability to bear emotional, as well as physical pain, differs from one individual to the other. An intolerance of depressive pain may lead an individual to resort permanently to splitting, to become superficial, lacking in warmth, as well as easily persecuted.

An adverse inborn balance between love and hate. When hate is strong relative to the capacity for love, a great deal of rage will have been experienced at an early stage of development. The damage done in reality and particularly in phantasy will be correspondingly great and may thus be felt to be impossible to make good. Consequently, the child may feel that just as he demanded that mother give up everything for him, so now if he cares about her he will have to become her slave. Attempts at reparation may also be so tinged with triumph, such as 'Ah! you are so weak, now I am better off, stronger than you are', that it defeats its own end and does not bring relief.

An over-strict conscience. As we have seen, Mrs Klein's work showed (1933) that aspects of the parents are taken inside the mind under the impact of extreme love and hate. Unless such splitting up decreases as a result of satisfactory development, the child continues to have in his inner world, internal figures of a very loving and very punishing nature (compare Rosenfeld 1962). Not only are the bad parents punishing, but the idealized, good ones are also felt to demand that the child be ideal and thus as intensely critical and disapproving of the bad aspects of his personality. This can lead to feeling too persecuted by guilt. To escape an overpoweringly accusing inner voice, he may react by rebellion like the delinquent or it may lead to violence and even murder. For instance, we saw the mother of the battered baby trying to get rid of the accusing voice of her baby by flinging him against the wall. Such persecuting guilt can also lead to suicide, i.e. trying to kill this inner complaining voice.

The successful outcome of depressive conflict—concern for others

If the individual's endowment is good enough and he has had good and stable enough relationships, he can deal with depressive conflict of love and hate for one and the same person by sadness, grief and reparation. He will then have reached a state of relative maturity in which his attitude has changed from seeing others purely in the light of their usefulness to him to one of being mainly considerate and concerned about others as well as the good parts of himself. Klein called this successful dealing with anxieties, *the depressive position* (1934). Winnicott, more aptly named it *the stage of concern* (1955). Out of concern for mother and her family may later grow the concern for the wider family of one's immediate group, one's community and eventually the plight of mankind.

Depressive anxieties, like persecutory ones, exist and alternate throughout life in all of us. They are particularly aroused when, in fact, we have injured or neglected someone, or a person who is important to us is ill or dies. Loss, whether temporary through absence, or permanent through death, further challenges our capacity to keep the loved person alive internally, to keep them in our mind and memory, protected from too much resentment and anger. Whenever we experience disappointment we are likely to doubt our lovability while any failure may bring with it the anxiety that we are unable to be constructive and that the bad parts of ourselves have gained the upper hand and shown themselves to be stronger than the creative ones.

3

Anxieties related to loss and mourning

Mourning as a reaction to different kinds of loss

We tend to think of mourning in the context of bereavement but, as Freud has pointed out, mourning occurs regularly as a reaction to 'loss of a loved person or to the loss of some abstraction which has taken the place of one, such as one's country, liberty, an ideal and so on' (1917, p. 243).

Some measure of grief and mourning occurs in all kinds of life-situations. Even quite ordinary changes such as a move to a new house, or area, involves sorrow at losing the familiar old surroundings and sometimes the closeness of friends. When we transfer to a new job we experience sadness at parting from our clients and colleagues; when we finish a period of training we regret leaving teachers who have enriched our minds and wonder how to manage without their support and help. Every step forward, as well as providing pleasure and new opportunities, means leaving something behind. We may turn away from it in disappointment and anger, but in as far as the past held good things which we treasure, we experience sadness and mourning at relinquishing them. Even children reaching adolescence often have deep feelings of regret that childhood has come to an end. In middle age we mourn the loss of youth and with it youthful ideals and ambitions left unfulfilled, and in old age we mourn the loss of energy and functions and the end of our own life. Facing the finiteness of our personal life and that of our loved ones is the most painful of the many processes of mourning that we have to encounter.

We shall now look at what happens in mourning, that is the feelings experienced when we lose someone or miss someone or face death, and how different individuals attempt to deal with this situation.

Freud's views on mourning

Freud studied mourning in order to gain insight into the depressive illness called melancholia, a pathological reaction to loss (1917). He pointed out that the distinguishing mental features of melancholia were the merciless self-reproaches leading to an expectation of punishment. He formulated the hypothesis that the melancholic's complaints were unconsciously directed against the lost one with whom the patient was identified. The other characteristics of melancholia were shared by the normal mourner. Both conditions had in common the following:

(a) an extremely painful dejection;
(b) loss of interest in the outside world;
(c) loss of the capacity to turn to a new love object;
(d) turning away from any activity not connected with the lost one.

Freud commented that it was only because we know the cause of this state so well and that it will eventually pass, that we accept it as 'normal' rather than an illness. He considered the work of mourning to consist in: (1) the testing of reality which proves over and over again that the loved one no longer exists, and (2) the gradual withdrawing of affect from the loved person at great expense of energy and time, ending after perhaps some months in a renewed ability to be interested in the outer world and to form new relationships. He related the intensity of pain and the length of time needed for mourning to the unwillingness to relinquish the attachment to a particular love object. Notice that Freud speaks of the 'work of mourning' to indicate that it requires a great deal of mental/emotional energy and effort.

Abraham's views on mourning

Freud's hypothesis that the melancholic internalizes the lost person, found confirmation in Karl Abraham's work, but the latter stated that this process also takes place in the normal mourner. 'The process of mourning thus brings with it the consolation "My loved object is not gone, for now I carry it within myself and can never lose it" ' (1924 p. 437). Abraham held that the normal mourner succeeds in establishing the lost one internally in a loving way while the melancholic fails to do so because of the degree of hostility towards him. The successful work of mourning which has commonly been regarded as the untying of the past relationship and detachment from it, was seen by Abraham to consist, in a way, of the very opposite : namely the firm establishment in the *internal* world of the *externally* lost one.

The internal experience of loss

Indeed this corresponds to what we experience when we part from someone we love and care about; that in order to preserve the good gained in the relationship, we need to keep it alive in our minds, i.e. internally. Let us listen to a sixteen-year-old boy parting from his case-worker. After she had told Jeremy that she would be leaving in three months' time because she was pregnant, he ceased to come to see her. The worker was worried and unhappy at having no chance to help him with his feelings, and was considering writing to him again, this time to say goodbye, when he turned up at the very last moment. In this last interview with her, he told her that he often thought about his grandfather who died three years ago; how he had imaginary conversations with him at night in bed remembering some of the things that grandfather had said, and thinking what he might say about present-day problems. Towards the end of the interview he spoke about scientists who reared babies in test-tubes, but he reflected that they also could push buttons and just destroy the world 'in one go'.

Jeremy illustrates well two ways of dealing with loss. He is capable of preserving his warm feelings towards his grandfather and therefore able to remember him with love and affection. This makes it possible to keep the wise counsel he once gave him and to listen to him as an internal adviser who helps him even in the present. The other way is to claim that mothers are not needed and babies can grow up independently in test-tubes. This part of Jeremy turns away from dependent human relationships as he did from the caseworker and annihilates her (as mother) 'in one go' at the moment of parting.

Klein: infantile roots of anxieties related to loss

Every time the baby feels a need for mother and she does not appear she is 'lost' to him. At first the baby's somatic-psychic needs are so great and overwhelming that they require a mother to be at hand to help to relieve them almost at once. Gradually the urgency for mother's immediate attention becomes less related to pressing somatic needs and more to psychic needs, i.e. to anxieties and inability to tolerate frustration. There are babies who scream unless continually carried about, or at least in auditory or visual contact with their mother. On the other hand, there are infants who as early as three months can at times lie waiting in their cots, happy, gurgling to themselves and reward mother with a smile when she returns.

How do we explain such differences? It would seem that these contented babies have been able to internalize a good sustaining mother and are able to hold on to this good relationship in mother's absence. To enable him to do so, the baby must (a) have had repeated good mothering experiences, and this depends both on the kind of mothering provided and on his ability to use it, and establish a good relationship internally, (b) not be so radically angered in the face of the slightest frustration that the good gained in mother's presence is destroyed at the moment of parting (compare Jeremy's pushing the button to destroy the world 'in one go').

The earlier outcome of the struggle to deal with loss determines how grief is dealt with later on. There are children who cannot leave their mothers and there are mothers who cannot let their children go without feeling rejected and unloved or else afraid that something untoward will happen either to themselves or to the other one. Such clinging behaviour is based more on hostility and fear of damage that will result from it than on love.

Infantile feelings are revived at every parting. Before a holiday, clients tend to miss, or be late for appointments and threaten to disrupt the contact previously established. They may complain about being let down, feel that the worker is unreliable and uncaring, be furious at being left in a needy state. Through their anger and disappointment, the worker may become devalued in their mind, or else they may feel themselves to be unworthy and too much trouble. When there is a question of transfer to another worker, they might be frightened about what they may have done to their worker and that the new person will be a punishing, stricter one. There is the real danger, or the concern, that what has been built up between them will be lost. The infantile part of the personality experiences such a loss as equivalent to losing a sustaining mother and father who made life possible in childhood, and as being left exposed now as then to want, terror, chaos and worry. As Mrs Klein (1963) pointed out, we are never truly alone, but alone with our internal world: either with feelings of helplessness, fear, terror and misery or, on the other hand, with some hope and inner security, founded on the expectation of love and goodness.

A child/adult who has not internalized a good experience or who at the moment of parting expels it, is therefore left with the persecutory anxiety that mother/worker is unloving, uncaring and inflicting pain, leaving him in a frightened state. Others have experience of a better relationship but are so afraid of the strength of their destructiveness that they fear whenever mother is not present, that she is lost through attacks, injury or exhaustion. When the child/adult has integrated the destructive parts of himself and has more trust that they are kept in check by the loving parts of his personality, he is more able to be alone, and out of concern for the loved person can allow her to lead an independent existence: to go her own way.

Holidays are a test of whether understanding and good feelings can be preserved by the client in the worker's absence. When enough good experiences have been internally established and there is not too much anxiety or hostility about being left, absence becomes a spur to development. Just as the infant's ability to let mother go and fill in time with play is an indication that the baby can be weaned—the child's ability to play alone or with others, an indication of his readiness for school—so the client's ability to make further progress during holidays while keeping good feelings towards the caseworker, shows that he has internalized a good relationship sufficiently to become independent of it externally. He is able to let

91

her have new clients (children) and use what he has gained for further enriching life experiences.

The client, just as the ordinarily cared-for child and baby has the opportunity to go through the process of repeated losing and re-gaining, seeing that his caseworker, like mother and father, survive, in spite of anger, external and internal attacks. Consequently, he gets some reassurance about the strength of love over hate. He has also the chance to be reparative by rewarding the parent/worker with growth and progress.

How different is the position of the infant or young child who is in fact left by his mother too early or too long, to face pain and worry. None of the reassuring conditions we mentioned above then exist. René Spitz's study of infants (1945) aged six to eight months have pointed to the fact that apathy, proneness to sickness and even mortality can result. John Bowlby's (1946 and 1953) and James Robertson's (1958) work on separation of young children from their mother have shown that the child goes through a process of mourning and that unless there is a good caretaking person, anger and despair can lead the child gradually to turn away from affectionate human relationships and instead become greedy for material things. Looking at these researches from a Kleinian point of view, we might say that the poignancy of the pain arises from the fact that the loss of the external mother shakes the infant's/child's belief in the goodness of his internal relationships and of himself. Without the reassurance of a mother who returns, the good internal mother is felt to be lost as well. Therefore he is left with persecution and despair sometimes so great that he loses hope altogether and thus the will to live.

Even the adult client, not yet ready to terminate, is faced with a severe crisis when the worker to whom he has formed a dependent relationship, leaves him. Months are needed to prepare the client and to work over the feelings aroused. Let us look at one such case in some detail.

Mourning the end of a relationship—transfer to another worker

The therapist told Miss C. right from the beginning that she would only be at the Clinic for five months. If help was still wanted and needed after this she would arrange for a colleague to take over. The client made a quick and deep contact with the worker and soon valued the work that was being done. Although the therapist referred at appropriate moments to the fact that she would be leaving, this was totally ignored. Two months before ending the worker had to miss an appointment. At the next interview the client remarked how warm and nice it was in the office; she was glad the worker was back; she had wanted to talk to her last week (on the missed Friday) quite urgently because she had a fearful row with her employer. He had told her off for being slovenly and producing messy work and Miss C. was not prepared to be spoken to in that way. He was 'horrible, cold, uncaring and inhuman. She wouldn't be surprised if he arranged for her to be isolated from the others and work in an office all by herself.' When she told the boss that no one had spoken to her like this before he had answered: 'It is about time someone did—you are no good at all'.

The therapist pointed out that although there had been previous tensions between Miss C. and her employer, she had not reacted like this before and that the outburst had occurred on the very day of the missed appointment. She interpreted that Miss C. felt the therapist to be cold, an uncaring person because she had left her. In an attempt to keep the good relationship with the therapist safe, particularly in her absence, it had been easier to feel angry with the boss instead. Miss C. now acknowledged feeling cross with her. She agreed with the interpretation that it was easier to hate if she could justify her hatred by claiming that the therapist was in fact unnecessarily cruel—then she need not feel guilt at hating the very person she so much valued. The therapist showed her client further that acting in an unreasonable way *outside* the treatment was in a sense punishing the worker, since it exposed the bad treatment she had been receiving. (She had time off from work to attend the Clinic.) At this the client became silent and thoughtful. She said she was hasty and impulsive. She considered herself lucky to have such a good job and she supposed that if she was to be given another chance she had better pull her socks up. The therapist acknowledged the client's sorrow at her anger, her feeling that she had been hasty in her judgment, for she knew that the therapist had made careful arrangements for her future treatment. Miss C. also seemed to imply that she was frightened she would not get another chance, namely that the therapist would not find her an able colleague to carry on the work. The therapist pointed out that the work the client had not wanted to do was to experience pain about missing her last week, and the feelings involved in facing the end of the relationship with her.

The working over of such feelings of anger, deprivation, of persecution and depression needs weeks and months of shared work. If this is not done, contact may be broken off prematurely, and transfer made hard or impossible. If the feelings can be understood, then the last few months may be most fruitful; provided the anger and anxiety is not too intense, the known limit of time can lead to a feeling of greater urgency and thus stimulate the wish to understand and work on the anxieties aroused and learn to cope with them in a constructive way. The therapist/caseworker has then the opportunity to help the client with feelings which are alive in the relationship now and have perhaps never been adequately dealt with before.

A transferred case

The Probation Officer Mr A., had prepared Tim for a long time for the time when he would be leaving, yet when Mr B. took over, Tim remained awkward and difficult. After some missed appointments Tim voiced his fury at having to come. He said it was Mr B.'s fault, that Mr A. was no longer there (very much like a stepfather who is blamed for pushing out the real father). 'Why did you take Mr A.'s job away from him?' After some time Tim said that Mr A. had been kind, a great guy, and he could not understand why he should have lost his job. Mr B. then told him that Mr A. had been promoted. Tim showed real pleasure and relief at this. It would seem that this information greatly reassured the boy that he had not damaged Mr A.'s reputation; on the contrary, he could feel pride that his worker had, in fact, a better job now. From then on he became more friendly and was able to co-operate with Mr B.

Bereavement

When someone dear to us dies we are left with the pain of loss and feeling of void, and also with doubts whether our hostility, lack of kindness and neglect have contributed to the person's death—or simply whether we could not have made his life easier and happier. We are also left without the comfort of being forgiven and loved in spite of shortcomings. Added to this are the terrible regrets that it is now too late to make good to the loved one what has been left undone in his lifetime. Hence the self-accusations, the guilt and the feeling of being persecuted by the dead and the living. (Such feelings occur to some extent in all mourning, but where the relationship has been unusually ambivalent they are stronger and may persist and stand in the way of re-establishing an internally good relationship to the lost one.)

Mrs Klein pointed out that the poignancy of the pain arises from the fear that the internal good object is lost as well as the external loved one. She says that the mourner needs 'not only to renew the links to the external world and thus continuously to re-experience the loss, but at the same time and by means of this to rebuild with anguish the inner world, which is felt to be in danger of deteriorating and collapsing' (1940, p. 321). Therefore the basis of his life, his belief in sustaining parents and his own goodness is shaken and he feels alone with chaos as in infancy. Close friends (or a caseworker) can help to counteract the mourner's feelings that all goodness has gone out of the world and that he is now left unloved and uncared for. On the basis of good external experiences he can start to re-build his inner world and the past.

Just as in infancy, idealization was a way of counter-acting feelings of persecution, so the mourner tries to re-instate the dead one by idealizing him, and finds comfort in recalling all the good qualities of the departed. In an attempt to protect the dead person against hostility (and against internal destruction) he turns it against those who are alive; or against himself. He may blame his state of deprivation on to the doctor, fate or an evil God, just as in childhood, the father might have been held respons-ible for temporarily taking mother away.

It is only with the gradual lessening of persecutory anxieties that there comes to the fore a real pining and sadness at the loss, and with it relieving tears. Out of the feeling of gratitude for the lost good relationship the wish may eventually arise to pass on the love received in the past by giving it to others. In this way the love and care received are not wasted, but continue to be alive inside us and of benefit to others.

A widow

Mrs T., aged fifty-five, had lost her husband seven months

prior to being referred to the medical social worker. The consultant of the out-patient department of the hospital felt that she was a lonely and unhappy woman who expressed her emotional difficulties through physical symptoms. He thought that she would improve if she could be encouraged to find some work and take up new interests. Mrs T. had seen the physician on innumerable occasions because of a persistent cough and various aches and pains. She had consulted the surgeon after passing blood, but nothing abnormal had been found. She had attended a Fracture Clinic and the Orthopaedic Department following an accident.

Mrs T., dressed entirely in black, appeared subdued and lacking in affect. She was wary of the caseworker, stressing that she wasn't fit to return to work. She was quite happy 'pottering about the house'. This meant spending her time tending her husband's clothing and possessions as if he were still alive; even his hat was still hanging on a hook in the living-room. The caseworker felt that her task was to provide support and allow Mrs T. to talk about her husband and their past life in the hope that she would be able to accept his death and mourn him. She also felt that Mrs T. needed to feel valued and cared for. The client appeared relieved when it was made clear that she would not be pushed into employment, and was eager to come and talk about the past.

Mrs T. came from a large Catholic family and had married a Jewish immigrant from Poland. She described her marriage as ideal, they had lived 'only for each other'. Mr T. had a slight stroke some years ago and later suffered from heart trouble. Mrs T. had worked half-time and had nursed him devotedly through his repeated bouts of ill-health. They had no children, Mrs T. having miscarried the one time she became pregnant. Her husband had wanted to adopt a child and she now felt guilty that she had not agreed. She had cut herself off from her family since her marriage, and the couple appeared to have had no close friends. After her husband's death, however, Mrs T. had spent a week with her married sister.

In the first place, we see here the need for the bereaved to be listened to and allowed to go over the past. There is relief that the caseworker is prepared to listen instead of telling her what to do. Mrs T. seems unable to accept the fact of her husband's death. She holds on to external belongings for fear of losing every part of him internally. It would seem that Mrs T. had a very exclusive relationship with her husband. This is borne out by her breaking all contact with her family and yet returning to it as soon as her husband died. We see it also in the absence of friends and the reluctance to adopt a child as if she did not wish to share her husband with anyone else. So her existence, built round one person, collapsed when he died and left her intensely lonely.

Quite soon Mrs T. began to ask the social worker for more frequent appointments. She was reluctant to leave at the end of interviews and repeatedly requested that the worker visit her at home. This behaviour made the medical social worker worried about Mrs T.'s dependency and afraid that the demands might be limitless if she gave in to them.

The caseworker kept to her previous arrangement and encouraged Mrs T.'s interest in evening classes. The client chose a course in Polish, which she enjoyed as something related to her husband. During the following months Mrs T.'s mood varied enormously; at times she was insightful and communicative, at other times she remained silent and complained of 'feeling rotten'. The caseworker made her aware that the silences coincided with 'feeling rotten'. At this time Mrs T. voiced a tremendous amount of anger against hospitals and doctors. They did not do enough to help her and had not taken her husband's illnesses seriously until it was too late. These thoughts had been bottled up for a long time. She appeared anxious about how the caseworker would react and greatly relieved when her anger could be accepted. She complained of 'feeling empty' and 'bad inside' and it became clear that physical symptoms got worse as soon as she felt angry and depressed at being alone, especially when she made a step towards managing better.

We see here a wish to keep her husband's memory alive, to learn his language as a way of coming closer to him and his background. While the caseworker remains sympathetic she is aware of Mrs T.'s infantile dependency needs and makes the limits of her role clear. This has the effect of arousing Mrs T.'s anger and at the same time reassuring her that the caseworker will not give in to her greedy demands. The relationship thus becomes safe enough for the client to voice her anger with the caseworker for not doing enough and with the hospital which she partly blames for her husband's death. Coming at this point, her physical symptoms seem linked to internal attacks on the absent one (for having to manage independently), and as a result harbouring an attacked, rotting, dying person; but note that she does not experience depression about her attacks but feels that *she* is ill and needing attention (i.e. she is identified with this sick internal object).

A month later Mrs T. considered whether she should become Jewish so as to be nearer to her husband in death, or whether to return to the religion of her father. This led to talking about her father's sudden death from a heart-attack when she was only nine years old. She had been alone with him and holding his hand when he suddenly collapsed and dropped dead. She described with great feeling her relationship with him which she considered to be very special. Although there were five sisters, she thought herself father's favourite. She told the worker of the shock and panic she had experienced at his death. She had not been able to talk about it to her mother but had been kept busy in order to help her get over the shock. (The doctor's suggestion now that she should work might have re-evoked her anger with her mother for not being allowed to grieve.) She was able also to express feelings of resentment at having been let down by her adored father and later her equally adored husband. At the end of this interview Mrs T. thanked the caseworker and said how helpful it had been to talk.

Here Mrs T. recalls the earlier loss revived by the recent one. It seems that she has never before fully mourned. She feels that she had a special exclusive relationship both with her father and her husband. There was never a mention even of her mother. One feels that she is a very possessive person who idealizes each relationship but turns to the next one when let down; we might speculate whether she turned away abruptly from her mother at weaning or when the next baby was born. We notice the turning away from her father's religion and the consideration of return when her husband dies. At the same time this also represents the wish to be re-united with them in death. If turning towards life is equated/ with turning away from the dead in hostility, rather than continuing the past relationship by transferring loving feelings into the present, then the past cannot be given up without severe feelings of persecution and guilt. This may result in slavish submission to and idealization of the dead which has to be continued indefinitely. The caseworker relationship gave Mrs T. an opportunity fully to experience mourning for both losses. The worker's survival after an outburst of hostility made it perhaps safer for the client also to voice her resentment and anger with the dead, and yet feel that they were not destroyed by it.

This interview proved to be a turning point in Mrs T.'s life. She began to look better, to consider wearing brighter clothes and to talk about joining a Club for widowed people. However, there were many ups and downs. Every step forward was followed by an upsurge of physical symptoms and feeling unloved. She would worry her caseworker by saying 'next week if I am still here' with the implication that she might die, have another fall, or commit suicide. The caseworker became worried that she might have to 'carry' Mrs T. for the rest of her life (as her baby). Some work had to be done to show Mrs T. her need to continue to be cared for and loved and her inability as yet, to worry and care about others when they left her.

It would seem that here the depressive anxieties are being pushed into and being carried by the caseworker: 'You worry, you feel concerned about me.' The client herself related the recurrence of threatening physical breakdown as a wish to be mothered: 'I feel lonely, then I get pains and so I can turn to people and ask for help.' The implication is, that if one is well people don't take notice of you, just as the good behaviour of children is sometimes felt by them not to pay as high dividends as naughtiness. Perhaps Mrs T.'s physical symptoms also implied guilt, as if her being alive, well and active meant triumphing over her dead husband. He was then felt to revenge himself by attacking her from inside.

Another turning point occurred some three months later. Mrs T. had often dreamt about her husband as alive, but in this dream she knew that he was dead. He appeared concerned for her and told her not to grieve for him. This she found most comforting. She now began to be depressed in a different kind of way, sad at the loss of a kindly husband and appreciating the good things they had shared. She invited the worker home to show her the photographs of their wedding and their holidays together. It seemed as if going over and sharing the past with her was a very important experience for Mrs T. She was also now ready to dispose of his clothes. She decided to be more active than before and use the life left her to help others. She began helping to run a Club for the lonely and elderly. She has kept contact with the caseworker whom she now comes to see only occasionally. Her accident proneness, her aches and pains have largely gone.

Her dream shows her acceptance of her husband's death as if for the first time she had allowed him to die. He in turn appears as an internal comforter, like a good parent, who is at the same time assuring her that he is not envious of her survival; on the contrary, he encourages her to go on with life. I think this indicates that going on living was experienced, as it is to some extent by all mourners, (Klein 1940), as a triumph over the dead person. If this feeling is very strong and persistent this leads to such guilt that the return to normal activities, and particularly enjoyment of any part of life, are interfered with. It is also of particular interest that Mrs T. can turn to the past now with less self-pity and more real sadness about losing a unique relationship with her husband. Going through the photo-album with the caseworker was a way of re-instating this relationship internally and feeling that her husband lives on inside here; perhaps even sharing him with the mother, as she never did in her mother's lifetime. On the basis of gratitude for the good relationship, and out of sorrow for her bereaved internal mother with whom she shares widowhood, she came to wish to be reparative and utilize the love received in the service of others.

Thus, the work of mourning can lead, as in Mrs T.'s case, to a deepening of feelings, greater empathy with others who suffer, greater integration of the destructive and loving parts of the personality : to emotional growth.

Brief examples of reaction to loss

Inability to mourn
Following the death of a dearly beloved and highly esteemed mother, Joan appeared light-hearted. She claimed that she was having the time of her life; people took such pains to be nice to her and she enjoyed the good restaurant food, the new clothes and the presents with which she was showered. Such failure to mourn shows

loss of the capacity to care and the concomitant strengthening of greed for material things and hatred of dependence on people.

Delinquency

Charles was an illegitimate child who lived alone with his mother and seemed very close to her. The mother had kept up the relationship with his father, and when he was twelve his parents married. The boy showed strong resentment at his father's presence and continued his opposition even when the father became seriously ill. He did not wish to visit him in hospital and was dragged along occasionally by the mother. There was a particular instance when mother urged him to go, he refused, and on the following day father died. Soon after his father's death, the boy joined up with a gang who broke into shops. He was nicknamed 'Smiler' by them because he was always solemn. He was backward at school and appeared to be dull and lifeless.

After a number of interviews with the Probation Officer, Charles voiced his wish to be caught and to be sent to an Approved School where teachers would be severe and punishing. He came to see that seeking of punishment was a means of eliminating feelings of guilt. He said that although he knew he did not in fact kill father, he still felt responsible for his death and wicked. He had sought to comfort himself by joining up with others who were equally bad. The Probation Officer helped him to see that his feelings of guilt related to his *wish* that his father should die and he should have mother to himself. The work done with the Probation Officer eventually resulted in lightening the boy's depression. He left the gang and blossomed forth as never before.

Seeking punishment and accident-proneness are common reactions to unconscious guilt. It is only when the real guilt and depression have been faced that the vicious circle can be broken.

A bereaved family

Christine V., aged two, died following a brief illness. After the initial period of disbelief and shock, the family sank into deep depression. Mr V. looked pale and drawn and when he came home from work sat staring into the fire, frequently dropping off to sleep. Mother was sleepless and full of self-blame. She was extremely angry with her husband for being aloof. Elizabeth, aged five, would not go to school and clung anxiously to her mother who, wrapped up in thoughts about Christine, tended to push her off. The little boy Peter, aged three and a half, was unusually active and noisy during the day but unwilling to be put to bed. He did not want to 'go to sleep' as he had been told Christine had.

This example shows that in addition to the personal loss of each member of the family, the inter-relationship of the different members is deeply affected by death. Thus, the mother feels deprived of her husband's support and fails to understand his way of mourning. The children too suffer a double loss. They do not receive the mothering and fathering they usually enjoy and so badly need now to help them with their own anxieties. On the contrary, they may feel that they must indeed be bad to be rejected by both their parents. Even their jealousy of the baby is strengthened by the feeling that mother and father care only about the dead one.

Mourning in relation to loss of function

As a result of a car accident, John at the age of nineteen sustained severe eye injuries. He remained cheerful and optimistic throughout months of hospitalization while the doctors tried several operations to save his sight. He was a model patient, loved by the nurses and doctors, always co-operative and in good spirits. His co-patients liked him because he had a fund of good stories; he even comforted his mother when she felt depressed about him.

It was only when John was about to be discharged from hospital, as no more could be done for him, that it became clear that he still clung to the belief that his vision would after all be restored to him. The medical social worker who discussed his future with him found that he was saving up to buy a car and planning to work in a drawing-office, as he had done before the accident. He totally ignored her suggestion that he take a course in Braille. At home he became irritable with his brother and sister who could read, romp about and go out when they pleased. His mother found John increasingly difficult as he required help in so many daily matters and yet accused her of treating him as a child.

The caseworker discussed his anger and despair with him, his envy of his siblings and his resentment at being dependent again. John demanded to have a second specialist examine him, claiming that it had never been definitely put to him that he could not regain sight. When the specialist confirmed the prognosis, he accepted the reality of his situation for the first time. Now he came to the caseworker with angry outbursts: 'Why should this happen to me?'; 'What have I done to deserve it?'; 'Why am I not allowed to lead as free a life as the others?' His feeling was that the accident was a punishment and life was unfair. At the same time John hated himself for having such thoughts and being so impatient with his family. The social worker conveyed that it was understandable that he might feel like this and that it was easier for him to say these things to her than at home. He in turn claimed that it was easy for her to talk, she didn't have to be blind like him and could enjoy her youth and life!

Later he came to reflect that he wished he had known this would happen: he would have 'drunk in' the colour of flowers and the beauty of girls and have visited more art galleries. He was angry with himself that he had not appreciated these more when there was still time to do so. Thus, he mourned the missed opportunities as well as the actual loss of a valued organ of perception. Gradually, as a result of the work of mourning, he became capable of taking a realistic view of what was still available to him and recovered his capacity to work, love and derive enjoyment from life.

Illness and accidents at any age may confront us with slow or sudden loss of abilities. Denial of the limitations imposed can only lead to a superficial adjustment which hides underlying persecution and depression. It is only when the work of mourning has been done and the anger, despair, and depression are eventually mitigated by love and courage, that the individual can go forward. If anger and despair predominate permanently, the individual regresses to an earlier stage of development, becoming self-centred, self-pitying, with a chip on his shoulder and begrudging others their freedom, or infinitely demanding of their time and attention. If the loss can be admitted, mourned and accepted with courageous resignation, a heightened appreciation of the remaining gifts and opportunities can lead to development in a different direction.

It is tragic if such a loss happens in childhood or early adulthood, when the youngster has not yet had the chance to unfold his abilities to the full or enjoy aspects of life from which he is now barred. Yet the possibility to compensate to some extent by learning different skills is greater than when the loss occurs in middle or old age when there is so much less flexibility of body and mind and the loss of function is experienced as the beginning of the end of life.

The person who has previously succeeded to some extent in dealing with ambivalence towards his parents for providing him with limited resources, who has begun to face his own limitations and can allow others, like his parents and siblings at one time, to accomplish things he cannot do, has a basis for coping with such loss.

Mourning the loss of youth and life

The ability to mourn what is irrevocably lost, to let go of others and to be resigned to inevitable limitations all play a most important part in the losses associated with ageing.

In middle-age the individual faces a *multiplicity* of losses; they occur either concurrently or in rapid succession:

(a) the loss of youth, awareness of which is brought home amongst other factors by children reaching adolescence;

(b) the loss of sexual recreative ability terminating in the menopause and in what has been called the male menarche;

(c) loss of opportunities for entirely fresh starts in career or marriage;

(d) loss of parental function as children grow up, become independent and leave home;

(e) loss of own parents through death, or facing their ageing;

(f) loss of contemporaries through untimely death.

All these demand to be mourned. They also have the effect of driving the individual towards a more conscious awareness of his own mortality.

Elliott Jacques in *Death and the Midlife Crisis* (1965, p. 506) puts it thus: 'The individual has stopped growing up and begun to grow old ... The paradox is that of entering the prime of life and fulfilment and at the same time prime and fulfilment are dated. Death lies beyond.' He shows that: 'The entry upon the psychological scene of the reality and inevitability of one's own eventual personal death is the crucial feature of the midlife crisis' (1965, p. 506). He states that the successful weathering of this crisis consists in acceptance and constructive resignation to the inescapable fact of personal death and that an ability to cope with facing external death depends on our being able to accept internal death, i.e. our own destructiveness. For our notions of death are coloured by the destructive feelings with which we have invested the external world and death.

Klein (1940) has shown that the unconscious meaning of death is derived from infancy: the baby's feeling-experience of being starved, abandoned, tortured, of going to pieces, all these persecutory anxieties are the equivalent of his experience of dying and death. It is this feeling experience which later manifests itself in conscious or unconscious fears of death. Death is then not thought of as a state of not knowing, an absence of feeling, but as if in death we fully experienced with all our senses the panic of helplessness in the face of immobilization, suffocation, being locked up, eaten up and disintegrating. Both Hannah Segal in *Fear of Death* (1958) and Elliott Jacques (1965) bring convincing evidence of the close connection between this infantile feeling experience of death as a persecutor and the sharp division in their patients' mind between an ideal mother/father and a persecuting one.

We have seen in earlier chapters that whenever the baby, child or adult takes back into himself some of his destructive feelings he becomes less afraid of an externally revengeful mother and instead sees her in a more realistic way. Jacques and Segal show how such integration of the destructive parts of the personality lessened the fear of death in their patients. Death was then no longer seen as hell or idealized as being lifted up into heaven—but could be contemplated with sorrow and resignation. Such integration of love and hate which lessens both idealization and persecution is the essence of what Klein called the progress from the paranoid schizoid to the depressive position. To some extent such integration begins in infancy and childhood, but Elliott Jacques states that the depressive position is worked over again in mid-life at a qualitatively different level.

As we have seen, any frustration or loss arouses hatred, persecution and depression. If the individual has had some previous success at coming to terms with such feelings, he will be better prepared to face the anxieties associated with death and mid-life. But if he has been unsuccessful, the crisis in mid-life may be greater. It may have been possible in the past to cope with loss by clinging to the vague hope that a new partner, a new job, a new country, a new house or a baby would provide the ideal satisfaction not obtained hitherto. Faith may have been invested in magical solutions, worries put off till the morrow and awareness of limitations blurred by relative success. When, however, the future itself is seen to be circumscribed and the life-span limited, the realization that frustrations and limitations are inevitable cannot be so easily denied; nor can the feelings of hatred and persecution. Life then is no longer felt to be all-bountiful, endlessly promising (like the ideal mother and father) but instead is experienced as cold, restricting (the frustrating mother), coupled with the uncaring ruthless avenger (the death-dealing father).

What impinges on us in middle age is the loss of the belief in an idealized object, and with that comes also the collapse of self-idealization. For disappointment and disillusionment bring to the fore all the destructive elements in our make-up, which may have been kept in abeyance before: rage at our helplessness in the face of inevitable death and illness; jealousy of those who enjoy greater happiness in their relationships, whether contemporaries or younger people (as in childhood the parents); and envy of those who are better off physically, materially, more creative, more successful. If love and gratitude for the good aspects of our existence can be brought to bear on these hating feelings, more depressive anxieties emerge: guilt at irreversible mistakes and omissions, regret at the waste of time and opportunity, sorrow at our lack of appreciation of what has been given to us.

In this way the encounter with death drives the individual back to re-examine himself and his relationship with his family, his work, his purpose in life. Such re-working of persecutory and depressive anxieties is bound to be extremely painful and may take years. It can, through the acceptance of life *and* death, love co-existing with hate, lead to fuller integration and thus to a strengthening and increasing stability of character.

Time seen not to be infinitely expandable, becomes more precious, and leads us to reconsider our system of values and priorities. On this basis, important life decisions may be taken, like having another baby or adopting a child while there is still time. Others embark on a more congenial sphere of work, while many people find new creative outlets. Awareness of destructive feelings and tragedy lead to greater tolerance of other people's feelings and more sympathy with their suffering. The finiteness of life makes relationships more precious, work more urgent, and can heighten the appreciation of beauty and goodness. Seeing life from a greater perspective can lead to serenity and wisdom. An individual of such emotional maturity ages gracefully and becomes an inspiration to others, of his own and the younger generation, and in this way indeed overcomes death; for he will live on in the memory of those privileged to have known him, or he may leave behind work which is of permanent value.

Some symptoms of failure to deal with loss in middle age

Depressive breakdown. There is a real possibility of a depressive breakdown to a greater or lesser degree in mid-life, or at a later stage, such as at retirement or after the loss of the spouse; other events, such as the last child leaving home, failure at work or an illness can trigger off the fears strenuously denied before. In Mr G.'s case, e.g.

it was the realization that he needed a younger partner to help him in his business which seemed to mark the beginning of his breakdown. He suddenly felt he could not work any more, was afraid of being impotent and behaved in such a suicidal way that he had to be admitted to hospital.

Alcoholism. The wish to escape from painful reality contributes probably to the higher incidence of alcoholism amongst older people.

Promiscuity. The need to assert one's sexual attractiveness and potency in the face of fears of ageing brings the temptation of extra-marital relationships and promiscuity. Affairs tend to be typically with much younger partners. Marital friction and divorce are common in middle age.

Competition with the younger generation. Envy of youthful sexuality and opportunities may find expression in the suppression of sexual drives of adolescent children, and so add to the friction between the generations. Alternatively, a parent may vicariously live through the child and encourage sexual adventures and irresponsible behaviour. In the work field, the need to be irreplaceable may encourage reliance on status and power rather than ability. It may also lead to the encouragement of the second-rate, who can be counted upon to flatter and remain dependent, and the subtle disparagement of really talented younger rivals.

Hypochondriasis. An over-concern about health occurs frequently. It is an expression, in physical terms, of the fear of internal and external death.

Increased greed. From the basic desire for food to collecting material possessions. In some cases this can also lead to petty crime. Shop-lifting in middle-aged women seems to be linked to the unconscious wish to steal mother's possessions (food equated with the breast, or articles representing feminine sexuality, e.g. handbags). Greed projected onto others leads to fears that the children are robbing the parents of their power, are merely waiting for their inheritance, or exaggerated worry that younger colleagues are wanting to push out their elders.

Summary

We have seen that we face many kinds of losses and states of mourning in the course of a life-time, from the grief at losing an ideal relationship to a feeding, holding mother, to facing the loss of life itself. Every loss means a severe test of our ability to preserve love and gratitude for the good mother, other relationships, life, and employ such good feelings to mitigate the feelings of hatred at frustration and limitations.

If in the long run anger and persecution, a grudge against parents/fate/God for giving us an insufficiently good life supervene, then love and effort come to a standstill. 'It is not worthwhile', or as someone said to me: 'What is the purpose of living if death comes at the end? It makes the whole thing pointless.' There is then the danger of a depressive illness and the risk of suicide. Another way of dealing with disappointment is to indulge in greed—'let us live for the moment for tomorrow we die'. This means giving up mourning and caring, a flattening of affect, a diminution of the capacity to love and involves *general character deterioration*.

On the other hand, we have seen that some losses are an inevitable part of our life experience and are indeed necessary for the attainment of mature adulthood. For the work of mourning can lead to a greater integration, strengthening of character, the development of courage, and to deeper concern for others as we come to appreciate the preciousness of others' and our own time of life.

4
Admiration and envy

Definition of envy

Melanie Klein defines envy thus: 'It is the angry feeling that another person possesses and enjoys something desirable—the envious impulse being to take it away or spoil it' (*Envy and Gratitude* 1957, p. 6).

Earlier, Freud had drawn attention to the girl's/woman's envy of the boy/man for possessing a penis (1933). Mrs Klein found that equally men were envious of female organs of procreation and that men and women envied others of their own sex who were superior in some way. Envy relates to the creative functions associated with sexual organs: not just the possession of a penis but male potency, also in the wider sense of male assertiveness and penetrating intellectual power. Equally, a woman's capacity to grow and nourish an infant and female intuition and sensitivity can become objects of envy. Envy may extend further to the couple who are creative together.

Envy has to be differentiated from jealousy with which it is often confused, both in every-day speech and in psychological literature. Jealousy refers to a relationship between *three* people, while envy needs only *one* other. Thus, a man may be jealous of the relationship between his wife and another man; or a child be jealous of the new baby because of the attention and love it gets from his mother. Hatred of the rival is secondary to wanting more love. In the typical jealousy situation A. wants more of what B. is giving to C. In contrast, envy implies that A. wants something that B. or C. possesses. Thus, the child who has to cope with the birth of a younger sibling will be envious of mother's ability to make or feed a baby. The outraged husband in the above example, if he is primarily envious rather than jealous, does not so much miss his wife's affection as feel angry and covet his rival's ability to be physically or mentally more potent and attractive. Such men regard women (and such women see men) as part of their possessions and seek to make conquests so as to have trophies to show off their superiority in rivalry with others of their own sex.

We must also distinguish between greed and envy. The greedy person wants more than his fair share so as to obtain maximum enjoyment for himself. Envy, which may appear in the guise of greed, has the additional quality of wanting more because one cannot bear the other person's greater enjoyment and wants to deprive him of it. In some cases the envious person does not in fact wish to possess what the other has, yet wants to rob him of his possession because of the pleasure the other derives from it. Such envy can extend beyond the grave, like the girl who said she envied the dead because others remembered them with love.

The envious 'dog-in-the-manger' attitude of : 'If I can't have more or better than you, I won't allow you to have it', is immortalized in the fairy-story of Snow-White : 'Mirror, mirror on the wall, who is the fairest of them all?' When the fairy-queen finds her beauty surpassed by that of the daughter she sets about to destroy her rival. I believe it is a custom in the East to attach a blue bead to a new-born baby so as to deflect the evil eye from the infant. Such envy frequently attributed in myths and fairy stories to goddesses, queens and bad fairies shows how women have always feared their mother's envy; this in itself is a projection of the envy they felt as little girls of their mother's beauty and creativity.

External circumstances stimulating envy

Envy arises in situations of obvious disparity of fortunes. The poor envy the rich, the weak the strong, the helpless those who wield power. Such a situation exists *par excellence* in childhood. The child feels weak and helpless in comparison to his parents who seem to him all-knowing, in control of themselves, and able to cope with any eventuality. Klein (1957) found evidence in the analysis of children that such feelings of envy originated in infancy, in the baby's relation to the breast. The breasts and other parts of the mother are associated in the baby's mind with food, security, comfort, relief of pain and all the life-sustaining functions. The mother is felt to be the source of goodness and of life itself and hence her possessions and qualities are most desired and envied by him.

Actual deprivation and lack of provision of satisfying experiences stimulate envy. This is particularly true in babyhood, for to quote Melanie Klein again: 'The infant's feelings seem to be that when the breast deprives him, it becomes bad because it keeps the milk, love and care associated with the good breast all to itself. He hates and envies what he feels to be the mean and grudging breast' (1957, p. 11). In the same way, later on in life, actual deprivation or misfortune greatly increases envy because the greater the need the more hostility is directed against the person who withholds help or those who are better off. While in childhood it is mother and father who are hated, these feelings are transferred later on to other adults or society at large. Altered circumstances, for instance, the loss of function, the loss of youth, bereavement, the barring from promotion, all can bring to light an envious part of a person's nature which had been dormant.

Envy can also be provoked by providing too much; for instance, a mother who proffers her breast whenever the baby cries; a father who always jumps to his son's aid even when the latter can manage on his own; and parents who, probably with the best of intentions, show themselves in the nude to their children are all, so to speak, parading their riches and superiority in a way that unnecessarily stimulates envy.

Admiration and gratitude versus envious spoiling

If there is adequate provision of care and love, and if the individual is not excessively envious, he is able to enjoy and be grateful for good experiences. Thus, the pleasure derived from mother's loving feeding and handling normally adds to the baby's admiration and love for her. The growth and the development of skills gradually diminishes infantile dependency and helplessness and so mitigates the feeling of envy. He begins to see that through taking in and learning he can grow to be gradually more like an older sibling and eventually like the parents.

The child or adult who can admire without too much envy feels gratitude towards those from whom he receives help. He is able to learn from their experience and example and will try to emulate the qualities he admires in them. In order to learn, the envious person needs to deny the source of food, of knowledge, of goodness and therefore no gratitude is experienced. Achievement may be felt as being due to his own resources, like the child who said: 'Mummy and Daddy didn't make me, I made myself'; or the person who does not so much want to know but 'to know better'.

Alternatively, the person attacks the help/food/knowledge. Some babies prefer their thumbs to sucking at the breast; others are sick after every meal without apparent physical cause; some children remain soilers and bed-wetters. (There may, of course be quite different reasons for such symptoms.) We see it in wilful destruction, in vandalism, as well as the more sophisticated verbal smearing attacks, mocking, 'spitting out' information; in sarcastic, biting remarks which may hide behind flattery, such as: 'You are the expert so I am sure you are right, but it looks to me like this. . . .' Consider also the client who says: 'I did exactly what you told me to and look what happened'; for example, following a discussion on the need to have less secrets in the family, Mrs C. went straight home and told her daughter that they had adopted her because her natural parents didn't want to keep her. Such misuse of the treatment situation was not based on ignorance or lack of understanding, but was related to spoiling the help given by the caseworker.

Inability to accept help

When goodness is attacked, it becomes spoilt and so no longer is felt to be so good, while what is bad becomes less so because less envy attaches itself to it. In this way no clear distinction can be made between good and bad, and judgment becomes confused. Nor can the attacked good and knowledge be incorporated successfully because of the badness attached to it and therefore it cannot contribute towards growth.

Envy may cause severe feeding and learning difficulties. The situation of being dependent, or being a learner, may become quite intolerable because feelings of inferiority provoke such hostility in relation to the person who is in the position of parent or teacher. Every gift becomes suspect as if it was designed to show off the superiority of the giver. The envious person is difficult to please and tends to find fault with everything that one tries to do for him. For example, I remember a boy who complained to his Probation Officer that his father did not write to him often enough. When the father thereupon wrote more frequently, the boy complained that the letters were too long and boring. Equally he felt that the interviews with the Probation Officer always came at the wrong time: 'If you had been here last night, we might have got somewhere.' This boy had been difficult to feed as a baby; his mother had spent hours trying to find a rhythm that suited him and months experimenting with different brands of milk before she found one which he would not sick up.

Since enviousness undermines the very foundations on which good relationships are built—for these include trust, co-operation, gratitude and love,—the person experiences deep despair about his inability to love and be lovable and in turn feels still more envious of the better relationships that others enjoy. In this way a vicious circle is set up.

Here is an example: Lesley, an attractive, intelligent, educated 16-year-old West Indian girl was taken into a local authority hostel after running away from home. The hostel was known to be one where the relationship between girls and staff was friendly and easy-going. Lesley said sarcastically, 'it is ever so nice' and complained about the 'too cosy atmosphere'. She wanted the hostel to be like a hotel where others fitted in with her wishes, without there being any personal commitments.

She rebuffed help and friendliness, saying she didn't want anyone's help—she could manage very well on her own: 'Why do you care?—I don't want anyone to care!' She generally created an atmosphere of discontent and strife in the hostel, objected to the few existing rules and got others to gang up against the Warden. Once, when left with young staff members, Lesley staged a rebellion, and got others to join in throwing eggs and tomatoes at the staff. When questioned about this, she stormed out of the hostel, shouting abuse and threatening never to return. Everyone got very worried about her safety and felt guilty at her having left,—while Lesley secretly crept up to her bed and went to sleep!

The staff felt helpless and useless, and such feelings were strengthened by the occasional signs Lesley showed of being capable of friendly and helpful behaviour. Considered in retrospect, this occurred only when someone else was in trouble or dire need.

She often drew attention to her colour: 'We are no longer slaves, you know' she exclaimed when asked to help with some domestic chore; 'I belong to the have-nots', she would say. These remarks, although a rationalization of her feelings of anger, rebellion and sense of inferiority, had the effect of making others feel guilty as if they were rubbing salt into the wounds of a suffering child, as if a little more patience, a little more encouragement and more consideration might bring about a quite different situation. It made them feel that in future they would have to treat her with more care so as not to upset her.

Although such considerations are very appropriate and may be helpful, in Lesley's case they were of no avail. The more helpful others tried to be, the more destructively envious she felt. It seemed as if Lesley manipulated them into being wrong, and played off one person against the other. She ruled the roost partly by her physical strength, partly by her sharp tongue; she managed to get people to quarrel and fight each other and would then sit back and enjoy it. Everyone found her exhausting to be with, could not stand her at times, and wanted to get rid of her when she 'got under their skin'. This in turn made them feel extremely guilty and the staff felt they had failed and were incompetent. Although they sensed Lesley's despair behind her aggressiveness, it finally seemed as if Lesley could not accept any other but material assistance. This, she said, was hers by right, while all other kind of help felt to her as if others were patronizing her and making her feel inferior.

This example shows clearly the destructive effect envy

has in a relationship of dependency and the desperate impasse in which both sides to it may find themselves. In therapeutic work, it may be one's understanding which becomes the object of attack. The result on the worker may be of feeling confused and incapable of coherent thinking. This happened repeatedly to a psychotherapist treating an adolescent boy. After every session with him she needed some time to 'find herself' again, sort out her thoughts and recover from his verbal barrage.

Here is a snippet from a session in which the envy of her maternal intuition appeared in an unusually open and direct way. After an interpretation which had brought relief and which he had momentarily acknowledged as showing how well his therapist understood him, he said sneeringly: 'How do you know what I want? How do mothers know what their children want? *I* don't know whether my cat wants Cat-o-Meat or Kit-e-Kat. A doctor on TV said that if a baby cries in a certain way, it means a particular thing.—Well, if you do know so much, you must have a script.' There followed an implicit plea for her to hand 'it' over.

To imagine that there is a blueprint for understanding instead of maternal intuition being a quality of mind which is creative from moment to moment, is a devaluation of a mental capacity. It carries with it the assumption that it is a *thing* which can be handed over (an inanimate 'breast' rather than an alive milk-producing one) and furthermore that ownership of it is being withheld out of spite.

The operation of unconscious envy

Envy is usually deeply unconscious. We tend to see it readily enough in others but be blind to it in ourselves. Yet, enviousness is to some extent part of everyone's nature, though some have it in a smaller measure than others. We tend to deny it in ourselves for it is felt to be such a shameful quality, because of:

(a) the meanness involved in begrudging others happiness and pleasure, derived from such things as popularity, success, wealth, health, youth or freedom;

(b) the spoiling of the very things we most admire and value: creativity, love, beauty, intellect, integrity.

Although the sophisticated person may pay lip-service to being 'ever so envious' we tend to ignore the stealing, destructive, spoiling aspects of these feelings: the belittling 'It's all very clever, but . . .' 'It is so easy for so-and-so' —'just luck'. Apart from the transparently back-handed compliments such as: 'He makes you look positively efficient', there are the more devious ways in which envy operates. The disparaging criticism, for instance, to show one is clever enough to spot someone else's weaknesses; the undermining of a rival's confidence; the spreading of rumours to injure someone's reputation; bringing insoluble problems to show that the teacher cannot do anything either; the imposition without gratitude on someone strong because 'he has it so easy anyway'. Often feelings of envy are transferred to whole groups: the rich, the upper-class, the whites, 'them'. Even negative characteristics may be envied: the carefree, the delinquent who gets away with it.

The envious person cannot enjoy the happiness of others without feeling sour. To avoid envy, he may unconsciously choose friends and colleagues who are not up to his standard; such a person may be capable of great devotion to others, as long as they are inferior or worse off in some way than he himself. Another way of dealing with envy is to claim that one is superior and better, even in situations where this evidently is not so. One little girl paraded in front of her mother with papers stuffed under her jumper exclaiming 'I have bigger busts than you!' She refused the food that mother cooked and would only eat what she could get for herself out of the fridge. Even so, she did not like the taste of milk, but when she mixed cocoa in it then she found it 'really nice'.

There are some children who do not admit to copying their elders, but actually *feel* themselves to be the ideal parent. For instance, one client recounted how she used to re-scrub the floors in her mother's house, especially in the presence of visitors, and how this made the mother feel furious because it showed her up as an inadequate housewife. Linked to this need to be better than the parent is a stealing attitude. Some people are quite unaware of this, like the student who produced as entirely new an idea which his supervisor had been flogging for weeks. Where stealing is the predominant way of dealing with envy, the individual can never feel that anything he has is really his own. The unconscious sense of having appropriated it from somewhere else makes him full of self-doubt, insecure; when success does come his way he may feel guilty, as if he did not deserve it, and also become afraid that others outside and the internal parents will now envy him.

Envy of the creative couple

Mr C., aged forty-five, a North-Country man of considerable charm, came for help because of intense bouts of anxiety and depression. He was worried that these feelings would gradually engulf him, for on occasions he had already been unable to get up and go to work. He could not understand why he was not happy for he considered himself the 'luckiest man on earth'. He was gifted and successful at work, married to an attractive woman with whom he was still in love, and the father of five talented and beautiful children.

His anxiety, as we came to see, stemmed from the feeling that such luck could not last, and that 'the gods must be jealous'. But it was not only heavenly interference that he feared; he was unable to let his own parents know about the extent of his good fortune and instead always stressed the difficulties and hardships. He was convinced that his parents resented the fact that his life was richer and happier than their own. Equally, he never told even his closest friends about holidays or other cherished plans, convinced that such schemes would miscarry if he did so. He harboured active phantasies of someone casting a spell and spoiling his designs. Thus it became apparent that he was persecuted by the fear of other people's envy.

His bouts of depression alternated with moods of light-heartedness. These had become more evident in the last two years, i.e. since his son had reached maturity and acquired a girl-friend. Mr C. now paid far more attention to his own appearance, and encouraged by the adoration and admiration of young people, became gay and debonair; he seduced a couple of girls and engaged in several amorous adventures. He had a vague notion that he might be stopping these girls from forming more appropriate relationships with younger men, but he was not aware that he was in this way competing with his son nor did he feel guilty at the suffering he caused his wife.

Interpretations about the denial of his ageing and his envy of his son, were ignored for a long time. Then a dream brought home to him the inescapable reality of these feelings. He saw himself standing at the altar hand in hand with his bride. Glancing round he saw his parents, wizened and wrinkled, frozen into immobility. In the second part of the dream *he* was sitting in the pew watching a young couple being married but as he looked their hands parted and the bridal bouquet withered. The two parts of the dream bring together (a) his envious looking which separates the loving couple and causes the death of the flowers, i.e. the children which will come out of this union; (b) the youth and happiness of the young couple, and his own marriage when he was young, was felt to be at the expense of the parents. His luck was felt to be the result of envious appropriation of his parents' ability and creativity. Hence he so much feared his son's maturity, for to him it meant that the end of his own life activity had come.

He now also understood why he always felt especially depressed in the winter. We found that he had identified with the weak winter-sun/father who is separated from the earth/mother and also with the mother who, deprived of father, remains cold, bare and infertile. The outer dead appearance of the winter landscape confirmed the fear of containing this unproductive internal couple, the parents inside him, stripped of warmth, enjoyment and creativity by his envy.

Some defences against envy

Idealization. If the admired person is put on a pedestal: 'You are so wonderful, I could never be like that', he may be felt to be sufficiently different to be out of reach of envy. This attempt to safeguard him from spoiling envy is likely to fail, for the more the other is idealized the more envy he is likely to arouse in the long run.

Devaluation. If the admired person can be experienced as 'no better than me' or only 'quite good', then he no longer possesses anything quite so enviable. This may make it possible to accept help from him. It also means that no guilt is experienced for the attacks which have reduced the other person to this devalued state, for they are felt to have been directed against an already worthless object.

Confusion and doubt. An alternative is not to know whether what is offered is good or bad; it is possible to avoid envy by always questioning the benefit derived or the value and goodness; this can be quite subtle and appear under the guise of being 'careful' and 'scientific'.

Denying others success. Sometimes the client actually feels better but does not report it because he does not wish to contribute to the worker's pleasure. He may actually make no progress or remain a misery, so that mother/teacher/caseworker need not be envied for being successful.

Arrogance and projecting envy. Display of one's own superiority, power, social connections, name-dropping, attractiveness, are all ways of trying to project envy instead of experiencing it. Some people, for example, always have to top a success story or a joke by one that is even better. Those adolescents who flaunt their sexuality making their parents feel old and pushed into the grave, may also be demonstrating their enviousness of more adult loving sexual relationships.

III

Gaining insight and applying it in the casework relationship

Introduction

In the opening chapters of this book we looked at the hopes and fears that might be brought to the casework relationship. Because such expectations are deeply influenced by earlier relationships, we studied the roots of positive and negative feelings and the conflicts arising from them in infancy and childhood. Klein did not put forward a completely new theory of development, rather she has extended and deepened the work of Sigmund Freud and Karl Abraham. She stressed the role of phantasy in building up an inner world, the interaction of internal and external factors; she differentiated between two main kinds of anxiety and found that these, and envy, profoundly affect the development of the individual's personality structure and relationships from the beginning of his life. It gives us an understanding of why some individuals do not reach the optimum of their potential. While anxiety, if not excessive, stimulates development,—intolerance to mental pain or exposure to too much pain too early forces the individual to adopt defences against anxiety which lead to inhibition, impoverishment, maladjustment or mental ill-health. The result is suffering for the person himself, or his environment, or both.

Klein has led the way to understanding psychotic

anxieties and thrown new light on character disorders and depressive illness. Though her work deals particularly with the early stages of development these profoundly affect the later ones. It should be noted that neurotic disturbances are rooted in a sub-stratum of psychotic anxieties, and that these continue to be present in the depth of the mind in everyone. Because of the infantile nature of some of these anxieties, they are difficult to grasp. The ordinary adult is hardly in touch with some of the more primitive phantasies and often finds their expression in concrete terms off-putting, if not frankly incredible.

In view of this, the value of written communications like this book, to the student of human nature, is probably very limited. Conviction as to the truth and usefulness of the concepts can only be gained in the actual working with clients. When adults in deep distress or young children talk 'like a text-book', then one becomes convinced that this is not 'just theory', but that these concepts have arisen out of working with and understanding of patients.

The value of knowledge of this kind rests on its being tested. It is useful to have a theoretical framework which seems to make sense of otherwise unexplained phenomena, but the way it is used and the extent to which it is applicable and true must be tried and decided on by each person for himself.

In the following chapters we shall look at attitudes which foster perceptiveness and therapeutic interaction and how we might use insight to avoid certain pitfalls.

1

Gaining insight

An example of two different approaches

Mr L. was seen by Miss B., a senior medical social worker, at the request of Miss A., a junior colleague. Miss A. had paid a number of home visits to Mr L. with a view to getting him to send his son to a Training Centre. The boy had been diagnosed as severely subnormal, unable to profit from normal or E.S.N. schooling, but the father had refused to allow him to go to a Training Centre. The worker had explained that the boy needed to go in order to mix with others and learn to improve his manual and social skills. She had pointed out the advantages of the Centre and the disadvantages of his staying at home.

She met with passive resistance. The father had insisted that the boy had been sick after going once and that he was better off at home with his mother. As Miss A.'s feeling of helplessness in the face of father's determined refusal grew, she found herself to be urging the father with more and more arguments. Finally, she felt the father was too angry with her for a useful interchange to take place and asked Miss B. to help. In her report she suggested that the father was unco-operative and possessive, not wishing to let go of his son or share his education with a teacher.

Mr L. arrived late for the interview with Miss B. The caseworker noticed that he looked tired and depressed. She made some comment on father maybe having found it difficult to come to see her. Mr L. agreed, saying that he had wondered whether there was any point in coming, but thinking it over he decided he would come and get another opinion. Miss B. listened without comment while father spoke of the improvements he had seen in his son over the last year. He said he would never agree to send his boy 'to a place like that for abnormals'.

The caseworker understood that the father had not been able to face the fact of having a mentally subnormal child and that he fastened on to every tiny detail of his abilities to prove to the worker and to himself that he was all right, or anyway would grow out of his handicap. To send his son to the Training Centre would show that he agreed with the psychiatrist's diagnosis and be tantamount to abandoning his hopes. Miss B. pointed out to Mr L. that he seemed eager to prove that his son was getting better. Thereupon Mr L. revealed that he was sure his son's disabilities were like an illness and that he was convinced that in another three years' time he would be like other boys. He was then able to talk at length of his phantasies about the nature and cause of the illness.

When father had come to a stop the caseworker commented on how tired the father looked and wondered whether he got enough sleep. Mr L. replied that worrying about his son kept him awake at night. For the first time he looked brighter, and said that no one had ever bothered to ask about his sleep before. He agreed with Miss B. that his fears about the boy's disability which he tried to keep out of his mind during the day really hit him at night.

Mr L. agreed readily to be seen again by Miss B. It was clear to the caseworker that before this father could send his boy to the Training Centre, his denial of the mental subnormality would have to be faced; not by simply confronting him with the facts, but by helping him deal with his underlying guilt and depression which drove him to deny them.

Now let us examine some of the factors that made the interview with Miss B. a helpful interchange and made Miss A. fail to establish a good contact.

Providing a suitable setting

What the second caseworker did was to provide a suitable setting which gave her client the chance to put his problem in a way that could lead to understanding. I am not speaking of the physical setting; this may be the worker's office or the client's home. Nor am I considering the agency's function; this is clearly important to bear in mind, but does not come within the scope of this book. I would like to explore the *mental setting* provided by the caseworker's attitude towards the client.

Open-mindedness. In the first place, Miss B. rid herself of pre-conceived ideas about her client. She might well have been influenced by Miss A.'s report and expected a rather stubborn, unco-operative client. Reports, while containing much useful information about what has gone before, can have this inhibiting effect and interfere with the spontaneous reaction and receptivity of the worker. If we want to get to know the client it may be more important to be unencumbered by somebody else's opinions (and one's own) than to know all the facts appertaining to the case. These can usually be left till later.

Interest in finding out. In place of pre-conceived ideas about what should be done, the worker showed interest in the client as a person. As well as paying attention to what was said, the caseworker noted some of the equally important non-verbal communications: the client's slowness, his lateness, his anxious expression, the drabness of his appearance, the deadness of his voice and eyes. She approached the interview with the attitude of an explorer wishing to find out, not knowing where things would lead and therefore taking all clues as relevant. Of course, there are some guiding lines based on experience and useful theories. But there remains the element of unpredictability, of variety of human response and the excitement of discovery. It would seem essential that each person be approached as a unique individual, and our task then is to find out how he, with his particular endowment and experience, is attempting to cope with the problems life poses for him.

Listening and waiting. In most cases the way we can best discover the client's problems and attitudes is to start by allowing him to make use of the interview in the way he wishes. Such limitations as arise must be seen to be essential to protect the client, the caseworker or the agency; but within such necessary limitations it is useful to wait and listen. For instance, Miss A. felt so pushed by the need to do the 'right thing' and by the desire to please the psychiatrist that she was exerting pressure on the father to send the boy to the Training Centre. This pre-formed objective limited her perception and indeed did not allow her to listen and see, nor did it create the right climate for Mr L. to want to communicate. Of course, it is often the client who imposes a limited aim—'You get me a house, that's all I want'. This, too, tells the caseworker a good deal about the nature of the client's relationship and what role she is asked to play.

The question and answer type of interview tends to inhibit freedom of expression. On the other hand, if we are prepared and interested in just listening for a while, the client can talk in a personal way. One can always ask relevant questions later on, and the answers are then more likely to be given willingly, in a fuller and more meaningful way. Thus, we get the opportunity to understand how this client feels about his problem, his relationship to important persons in his life, what his phantasies are and also the nature of his relationship to someone who is there to help. Miss B. came to the interview with no definite idea as to what was to happen there and then. Instead of telling the father what to do or questioning him. She was free to listen and observe and so find out why Mr L. behaved in this particular way. The father felt that this caseworker accepted and respected him and cared. This enabled him to convey his misery and the ideas he had developed, in order to give substance to his precarious hope for his boy's future.

Taking feelings and phantasies seriously. It will be recalled that Mr L. talked about the little improvements he had seen in his boy. Although the evidence hardly seemed to support father's statements, the caseworker did not at once point out the discrepancy. Rather she took it to be an indication of this father's desperate need to hold on to the slimmest hope. It was the wish to convince her of the boy's normality which Miss B. chose to comment on. This might be said to imply a question and the father took it as such and went on to talk in greater detail about his phantasies about his son's state of mind. The worker did not jump down the father's throat with a remark like: 'Come, come, now, you know it is not really like that'. While being quite clear in her own mind about the facts of the situation she accepted that this client at this particular moment of time had to cling to his phantasy and for the present was unable to accept the painful reality. (There are of course certain situations where it is necessary and desirable to confront the client with the reality situation there and then; for example, if a patient needs to be admitted to hospital, there may be little time to work through the distress. This may have to be done at the same time or subsequent to taking action.)

Miss B. realized that the work required was not to contradict Mr L., but to understand the need for the denial of reality and so she enquired about father's sleep and got to the feelings of worry and depression. We see how with every comment Miss B. made, she carried the relationship and understanding one step forward. We might say that the client, if he were to put his feelings into words, experienced something like: 'This person listens to me, she does not impose her ideas, she does not make me feel little, bad or mad; she accepts my feelings and ideas as something important to me, yet she is not dominated by them, and can still think independently about my problems.'

How do we know what others feel?

It is worthwhile to reflect on how we know what others feel. Most commonly we think what we might feel if we were in the other person's position—if I were in your shoes—in their mind and body. We feel we can do this because we share certain basic human attitudes, motivations, emotional reactions and we use our imagination to fill in the rest. For instance, we may feel that if we were Mr L. we would be very disappointed at having such a son. We might go on to think that he must make very great demands on the parents' patience and that we, in Mr L.'s position, would be eager to have a teacher share the responsibility for his education and glad to have the boy looked after for some hours every day.

Such empathy is useful up to a point, but is only a rough guide and may lead us to make quite wrong assumptions. We can only *guess* what it must be like to be that father and our guess is based, amongst other things, on our personal capacity to deal with disaster and a disaster of this particular kind. We may find it, according to our own psychological make-up, easier or more difficult to deal with a mentally subnormal than a physically handicapped or psychotic child. Our judgment, based on 'putting ourselves into someone else's shoes', will be wrong in so far as we are different from our client and yet assume that he is like us. Miss A. felt that if she were in her client's position, she would have wanted her boy to go off to the Training Centre. Possibly Miss A. is more able to face disappointment, more rational, and on this basis expected the same of her client. Alternatively, it may be that her way of dealing with anxiety is by action. In either case this kind of 'knowing' barred the way to understanding a person different from herself.

What then is the alternative? Miss B. showed us that it lies in a *receptive attitude*; taking in what Mr L. looked like, what he said in so many words, what was expressed by coming late, his posture, his face, what mood and feelings were put across and what *the worker was made to feel*. Instead of saying to herself 'What would I feel like in Mr L.'s situation?', she waited to see what happened and what Mr L. actually felt like and also took note of the feelings and ideas evoked in herself on the basis of such communications from the client. (Compare chapter on Transference and Counter-Transference.) It made a picture inside her mind, which, if she were to think it out and verbalize it, might be something like : this man cannot bear having a mentally subnormal son and he has developed a theory in order to allow himself to go on believing he will be all right. But his denial of the facts is not complete. His sleeplessness which I guessed at by seeing how tired he looked, and which he confirmed, shows that doubts nag and worry him all the time. He looks miserable and it seems he cannot face the facts, because he cannot bear the despair and depression if he lets himself fully know them.

'Putting oneself into the other involves imaginatively using one's mind as if it could be inside the other person's. This is called, in psycho-analytic language, projective identification, because it involves feeling like the other person by projecting into him in phantasy a part of oneself; for reconnaissance, so to speak. Being receptive, on the other hand, taking in, means using one's mind as an instrument sensitive to the vibrations and echoes set off in it by someone else's projections. This receptivity is not to be confused with passivity. Before we can register what the other person is like, we have to be wanting to find out—to be attentive, as well as open to receive communications. It is an attitude which in its diffuseness and open-endedness bears more resemblance to a radar screen than a search light.

W. R. Bion (1962) has illuminated the nature of this process further. In becoming aware of the feelings engendered in him by his analytic patients (whilst being in control, and in touch with his own feelings), he realized that he was responding to a kind of communication, that he was made to feel that state of mind which the patient wished to communicate or else could not tolerate in himself. Bion states that such phenomena are convincingly explained by Klein's theory of projective identification (1946); namely, that there exists a phantasy that it is possible to split off a part of one's personality and put it into another person. This mental mechanism, he says, is used either for communicating or for getting rid of an unwanted bit of the personality. Not only does the mechanism operate in phantasy, but it results in modes of behaviour and action which in actuality evoke the desired response from a receptive person. He believes that from the beginning of life the baby is capable of acting in a way that engenders in the mother feelings that he does not wish to have or which he wants her to have. This behaviour also enables the mother to understand her baby through receptiveness to that aspect of his psyche which is projected into her.

While such taking-in is less likely to produce entirely false conclusions about others and is thus a more helpful attitude in dealing with clients than putting ourselves into the client's situation, the worker's ability to be receptive depends on her being in touch with feelings. A deficiency in awareness of her own feelings in any particular area would lead to overlooking relevant clues, or distorted perception, while an inability to deal with anxieties may leave her overwhelmed by the client's feelings. This will be discussed later.

The theory of being receptive to what the client communicates by projection could be said to provide a theoretical explanation of what we call intuition (or appropriate counter-transference). It is an extremely helpful one because it makes us aware that the effect a client has on us may be a valuable indication of the kind of feelings he *wants* us to have. These may be happy ones, but more often he communicates and deposits with us the feelings of despair, depression and fear which he cannot bear. This throws light on why therapeutic work of any kind is so extremely exhausting. To be the bearer of feelings others find too hard to tolerate is indeed a heavy task!

This kind of communication is often non-verbal, accompanying and sometimes contradicting what is being consciously communicated. Alternatively, we are made to feel the unwanted part of the client during a silence. Most people find silences difficult to bear and the worker tends to experience it as a sign of hostility. While this is often so, it may equally be a communication of despair of being accepted and understood; or an expression of a wish to be understood without words, like an infant; to be in one with the other person; or it may stem from the desire to evoke worry and concern. The nature of the communication must be divined by the worker from all the clues available and by being aware of her counter-transference feelings.

It would seem that we are discussing here a process quite different from repression. While repression is an internal suppressing of emotions causing conflict, projective identification has to do with pressing the unwanted feelings out of one's mind and into someone else.

We are, of course, all familiar to some degree with what is here described, for we know that fear and depression are 'infectious' and that it is hard to be for long in the company of, for instance, a severely depressed person. It is not a sufficient explanation to say that we have the same fears and states of misery as the client or get frightened and depressed out of sympathy, although these factors are bound to be operative to some extent. In so far as we are prepared to be receptive, we feel that the demands made on us *are* a burden. 'Grief shared is grief halved', the wish of the miserable person to 'unburden' himself, and 'it's such a relief to be able to tell you', all these statements express the psychic experience of pain being capable of expulsion and the need to have someone bear it with us, or for us. The theory of projective identification and our vulnerability to penetration by another person's mental pain, being made to be the carrier of it, gives this experience depth and purpose as well as explaining its therapeutic importance.

2
Therapeutic interaction

Introduction

We have gained a picture of emotional life in a constant state of flux: impingement of external and internal stimuli produces continuously changing moods and feeling states. There are anxieties arising from within and these in turn may be sparked off by physical stress, painful events and upsetting experiences. The ability to cope with these occurrences depends on inner resources and their availability at that particular moment. A person may actually rise to a crisis by greater effort and discover unexpected strengths. Alternatively, he may already be strained to the utmost and any additional burden becomes too much: it is likely that there is a potential breaking point for even the most stable person. Looking on the positive side of the scale, a drive towards integration exists as part of our inborn equipment; development of physical, social and mental skills help in the mastery of anxieties and chaos; happy circumstances, warm and stable persons in our environment, provide the opportunity for enriching experiences and development.

Understanding of these constantly changing states of relative integration and disintegration and growth on the basis of coping with anxiety, highlights the need for, and the benefit that can be derived from the client/caseworker relationship.

The caseworker's first contact with the client more often than not occurs when the client is under special stress or in an acute crisis. His anxieties are, therefore, likely to be heightened, and he may accordingly appear more disturbed, or more defended against anxieties than he does at other times. The same condition provides an optimum point for therapeutic intervention, for it is when anxieties are 'hot' (or the client 'cold' with anxiety) that he needs help most and the caseworker has the greatest chance of being therapeutic by making herself available to the client's mental pain. If she can provide an outlet and act as a receiver for the excessive anxiety which the client cannot at that moment cope with, it will bring him relief. It also gives the more mature part of him the chance to come to the fore and recover whatever ability he has, to understand, work over and eventually integrate the painful situation, instead of acting and thinking defensively. This might take time and requires the case-worker's ability to be patient, thoughtful and contain emotional pain.

Understanding, holding and containing mental pain

Let us now look at the therapeutic interaction in greater detail. In the example quoted in the previous chapter, the caseworker was able to see and verbalize the client's despair, and by doing so showed that she could accept such feelings. This will have meant to the client: 'This person cares. She can bear to look at my despair without being afraid of it and seeking ways of avoiding it. She is someone who can feel despair and not break down under it and this gives me hope of despair being tolerable.' The caseworker's attitude further indicated that talking about problems may be a way of finding a solution. In this way she has accepted Mr L. as a person, capable with her help of looking at the distressed parts of himself, not in order to indulge in despair but in order to examine and work on it. A complicated process of communication has taken place which brought relief and a glimmer of hope to the client.

What the client takes back into himself is the possibility of a difficult, despairing, anxious part of himself being held by the worker. This is the role that a good mother performs for her child. D. W. Winnicott (1955) has drawn attention to the great need of the infant to be held both physically and emotionally by the mother: this holding, as Winnicott says, 'facilitates' his psychic development, because it allows a time-span in which to learn to cope with his anxieties.

Klein's understanding of the complex mental life of the baby, his limited ability to contain the destructive elements of his nature, his need to use his mother as a person onto and into whom he projects his aggression and anxieties, has clarified the nature of the holding function and why receptivity and holding are of such vital importance. It is to take care of, to hold and to contain the baby with his terror.

A dynamic process goes on if a receptive person is able to listen, understand and contain mental pain. We do not yet understand all the processes that make this a therapeutic interchange, but two elements in it have been explored by W. R. Bion (1962). One is that the client, finding his anxiety, aggression and despair accepted and contained, is enabled at a feeling level, to realize that someone capable of living with the feared or rejected aspects of himself, does in fact exist. These parts of himself are thus not all-powerful and therefore they become less frightening; they can then be felt to be capable of being bound by love and concern. Such an experience with an understanding, caring caseworker, who yet is not overwhelmed by the client's feelings, makes it possible for the client to introject a kind of container/ mother holding this aspect of himself. Anxiety is thus modulated and his internal world becomes enriched, more manageable and stable.

This model is based on an infant being held both physically and emotionally by a mother. For instance, hearing her baby's terrified screams mother responds by picking up, holding and carrying the baby, her arms around him forming a cradle which expresses that he is not falling to bits, but being held together and saved. Note that it requires both the mother's understanding of his fear and a response in terms of physical handling which meets his emotional need.

Adults usually require holding only in the mental sphere, for they are almost always capable of managing their own affairs once their emotional needs have been understood or relieved. Only in the rare cases is it necessary to provide a setting in an institution which provides an external holding environment safe enough against destructive urges. In some cases, as in the problem family we looked at, action alongside understanding is essential; but if the worker is taking action based on her own need to do something, not understanding that the client's urgent demands arise out of inner emotional urgency, the client may feel more despairing, or else feel that he is confirmed in his defensive attitudes.

Failure to respond appropriately, whether with a baby, child, or an adult, leads to a feeling that aggression, depression or terror cannot be borne by the other. It continues to be felt to be an omnipotently powerful force that cannot be circumscribed or bound. It comes to be experienced as endless and unspecified, or, as Bion (1962) puts it, a 'nameless dread'. On the other hand, the mother/therapist who can accept and hold his terror, makes it possible to establish inside his mind an experience of terror that can be borne and so alongside of terror and despair there is hope. It is an image of a relationship of a frightened 'baby-part' held by a mother, or, as one of my patients said, 'an egg inside a basket'. The image does not deny or ignore the reality of the terror as it does in repression, but sets it in more manageable proportions because of the equal reality of the love and support given by the mother/worker who goes on holding, instead of panicking, disintegrating, juggling him out of his fear, fobbing him off, or deserting him.

A child and adult will be inspired by the example of those who can courageously endure anxiety and pain, while his attempts to deal with the frightened and aggressive parts of himself will be undermined by the weakness, the hypocrisy and the superficiality he finds in those who are in the position of parents and authority. Caring, containment, courage and endurance, are probably the basis of improvement in so-called supportive environments and non-directive supportive therapy.

Related to, but additional to containment of mental pain there may be a second factor. That is the parental capacity, not only to care and worry, but to think about, to clarify, differentiate, give a vague feeling a name and link it to what is meaningful, and so modulate pain. Bion speaks about the mother's 'reverie', i.e. her capacity to think lovingly about her baby and its feeling state. He suggests that this fulfils a function equivalent to a kind of mental digesting which transmutes unendurable distress into something more defined, thus making it safer to experience. Here is a simple example of this: a woman complained of a pressure on the top of the head, which she was sure would crush her. There was no medical reason for this. The first task was to explore what this pressure felt like, to see that it arose out of a worry experienced in a physical way, then to explore the nature of the thoughts that she was afraid would crush her down if she let herself know them. This patient commented one day, 'I send you my dirty laundry and it comes back clean, stacked and orderly'. It is a great relief when instead of experience a general feeling of doom, but to be able to understand what it is about. Equally, it is helpful to be able to differentiate between depression and despair, and despair and persecution, and understand all kinds of different shades of feeling. Some mental order is brought about by correct naming and identification of feelings and they then become more manageable instead of being vague and limitless.

Different kinds of holding of emotional pain

Holding doubt and fear of the unknown. Most of us have had the experience of being thanked by a client for a very helpful interview in a situation where we feel we did not do anything. Perhaps the client had got stuck over a problem, and as a result of the interview he has begun to sort it out, and some dramatic improvement has taken place. I would suggest that the caseworker *has* done something and underrates its value to the client. She has listened attentively and with understanding. Perhaps she has shown an appreciation of the difficult situation the client was in, or not agreed to blame someone. She might have asked a relevant question here and there which helped to clarify the issue.

Here is a brief example: Mr and Mrs G. told the caseworker that their ten-year-old girl had been wetting the bed for the past 1½ years. Her school complained that she was lacking in concentration and the parents said she had become uncommunicative. After they had given a fairly full history, the caseworker asked whether they could think of any important event just prior to the onset of her symptoms. It then emerged that the grandmother, to whom the girl had been deeply attached, had died. 'We never thought of that before,' they exclaimed. It was as if a light had been suddenly switched on and they could now work out for themselves, that probably it had been a mistake never to talk about grandmother's death.

They had omitted to do so, because of their own distress and because they feared to upset the girl. Now they wondered whether the girl took their silence to mean that they did not care about grandmother. She must have felt cut off from them, left alone with her grief, fear and suspicions. A month after this interview took place, they wrote saying that they had talked to the child. She was now much happier and the bedwetting had stopped; this symptom seemed to have replaced tears.

Notice that the caseworker did not offer her opinion or advice. She did not intrude on the parents' thinking and looking for understanding, but she provided a setting where they were listened to, and able to listen to their own thoughts, explore and look for clues. This activity, I think, involves the client in a certain amount of anxiety: he has to face 'not knowing' and this brings with it the fear of becoming confused and finding no answer, lost in doubt and despair. As I see it, the caseworker, by acting as a container for these fears and showing by her attitude that she is not omnipotently knowing either, makes it possible for the client to accomplish a task which he cannot do on his own.

Holding over a period of time. If the problem is of long-standing and extensive, it cannot be expected that solutions are readily available or psychic change come about, except slowly and with many relapses. This will tax the client's ability to stand doubt and despair about the usefulness of the therapeutic work. The caseworker will find that she, too, is made to feel hopeless and may well be tempted to give up. She may underestimate the length of time it takes for the painful emotional work to be done and the value of her continuing to provide a source of hope and strength to the client. For the client needs someone who has sufficient patience and tolerance not to give up; someone who is available to turn to, who knows about his past, his assets and deficiencies. The security that the caseworker provides as a caring, holding parent, may be the only one available to him at that period of life, or the only one he has ever known.

It is important, however, that the caseworker should not encourage dependency; she may be tempted to do so because of the satisfaction she feels in finding someone so dependent on her. This would hinder the·client's need to grow up and be able eventually to do without help. It is essential that the caseworker recognizes the client as a person capable of, to whatever limited extent, adult attitudes and responsibilities. For it is within the context of the worker's alliance with the mature part of the client that the weak, distressed or delinquent parts can be looked at, held and eventually integrated by the client.

Containing conflict. Conflict may be experienced by the client mainly internally, or acted out in his relationships with others, or a mixture of both. Valuable work has been done by caseworkers with marriage partners and whole families. In such cases she acts as someone who contains and holds the family together, by being able to contain their conflict. By providing this framework it becomes safe for them to air their grievances, express their hostility and explore the assumptions they have made about each other without feeling that the relationship is bound to break up. Communication, exploration and understanding may thus be established.

This is to be distinguished from abreaction which I understand implies the acting out of impulses. Nor is the client stimulated to indulge in infantile attitudes. The therapeutic work described here lies in the tolerance of expression of feelings in words and thought and only to a limited extent in behaviour. The caseworker is working in alliance with the sane, mature parts of the client and the infantile modes of thoughts and feelings are brought out for review, to be understood and worked on. In group and individual therapeutic work alike, the different parts of the personality or the way these are expressed and projected on to different members are being looked at: the loving and hating; the idealization and the persecution; the omnipotent and the helpless; the responsible, caring and the irresponsible, careless ones. If the caseworker is aware that all these form parts of a whole and can tolerate the conflict that is produced by their co-existence, her ability to contain these opposites and go on caring for the whole person/family/group, in spite of its bad aspects, will make it easier for clients to contain conflict inside themselves and so function better in their relationships with each other.

Containing anger and helplessness. A different degree of holding operates when the client uses the caseworker not so much as a container for excessive anxiety, with a view to it being modulated by understanding, but in order massively to get rid of an unwanted part of himself. In such a case he will behave in a way that produces helplessness as well as suffering in the caseworker.

Here is an example. Mr H.'s child had been removed from home by Court Order because of neglect and non-attendance at school. The caseworker felt that her task was two-fold; she had to help the mother deal with her feelings and to ensure that the child was not cut off from contact with his mother. She visited the child in the Children's Home and talked to him about his mother, because Mrs H. refused to go and see him herself.

Whenever the caseworker called on Mrs H. the door was closed in her face. The worker felt rejected and completely helpless. She recognized that she was being made to experience just what the mother might have felt when her child was taken from her, angry and impotent to do anything. She saw that this was a repetition of this mother's pattern, for by claiming that she could manage on her own and railing about being bothered, she had succeeded in making several previous social workers feel useless and give up. This caseworker thought that if she, too, failed, mother would feel herself to be destroying yet another person who was trying to help. On the other hand, if she attempted to force her way into the home or pursue the mother too hard, this would confirm mother's belief in an interfering, punitive authority. (This situation corresponds to that of a mother who, finding that the child turns away from the food as if it was poisonous, forces it down his throat, while a more confident mother is capable of tolerating rejection and can allow the child the chance to test out reality and find his way back to a more trusting relationship.) The worker's panic at her helplessness in the situation made her aware that these were the feelings the client could not tolerate and had projected into her; but how could she get in touch with the needy part of mother? She wrote a letter to Mrs H. saying she hoped this was not the end of the relationship; that she realized that mother must be very angry, but also very alone with her feelings (mother in fact lived alone, had been deserted by her husband years ago, and had no friends). When the worker called two days later at the appointed time she was admitted. Mother hurled insults at her and shouted in rage: 'You are welcome to take all the children away!' The worker sat through this, feeling the full impact, but remained in control of herself. Eventually she could say to the mother that she seemed to be feeling that in taking the child away, some very fundamental bond had been destroyed and that she feared that the relationship to him could never be repaired. Notice that she took up the client's *anxiety*, by-passing the defence against it. Later she pointed out that in closing the door on the worker and by not visiting the child, she was acting in a way that was hurtful to herself and indeed made an end to the relationship with her child, but that she knew that mother wanted something better for herself and her child.

Containing guilt and depression. Mr and Mrs K. came to see the social worker in deep distress when their child was known to be dying. They expressed doubts about the care the child had received in hospital and this was followed by self-recriminations at not having recognized his illness early enough. The parents, particularly the mother, formed a very close, dependent relationship to the worker, who helped them over the first period of shock and depression. Later on, the caseworker became concerned about mother who was e.g. accusing her husband of not mourning: he could go to sleep whilst she lay awake at night thinking about the dead baby. She worried, too, that the mother was overlooking the needs of the other children. For instance, the day after the funeral the mother insisted that the three-year-old went off to school, though he clearly showed that he was anxious and wanting to stay near her. A few weeks later she did not want to buy presents for the eldest girl's birthday. The mother obtained a good deal of relief by coming to see the social worker frequently and being able to get in touch when she needed to. She talked mostly about the baby, the difficulties she had experienced in giving birth and feeding him, and her inability to have more children.

Two months after the death of the baby she announced her intention to adopt a baby immediately. She said this would make up for the lost baby and it was the only way to prove to herself that she was a good mother. The caseworker tried to put it to the mother that such a replacement was in order to escape the painful feelings of doubt about herself. The client remained adamant and threatened that if the caseworker did not support her application for adoption, she would have nothing more to do with her; talking was not enough.

Although there were moments of being able to get in touch with guilt, grief and depression, the client drifted away from the caseworker. The husband seemed to support the mother in this. The mother took a job, reported that she felt capable and happy, but sounded frantic when she rang the worker. The caseworker felt increasingly unhappy, recognizing that the precipitate action was an expression of the inner urgency to do something in order to escape intolerable feelings and was worried that mother might be heading for a break-down. She attempted to visit the client at home, but the mother was always out.

At this point the caseworker felt deeply depressed. What had she neglected to do? Where had she failed? If this could happen was she any good in her work? How could she have avoided such a disastrous outcome? In other words, *she* now felt that she had lost *her* 'child' and all the feelings of self-blame and guilt and depression that go with failure and loss. In addition to her own suffering, she felt worried on behalf of the client. She experienced great hopelessness and despair; yet on the basis of her ability to *just* bear this painful experience, she had some hope that the client had got some relief by having projected these feelings. She also hoped that if she kept in touch by letter, thus showing her tolerance and ability to survive, the client might find some comfort and eventually a way back.

Providing a firm containment. A person may rid himself of his ability to love and be responsible so as to avoid conflict with the destructive urges from within. He may then behave in a way which we cannot accept or tolerate because that would be tantamount to colluding with his cruelty or delinquency. In our behaviour and verbalization we need to act as firm parents and at the same time try to restore the good aspects of his personality to him. Such a client taxes the caseworker's belief that there is anything worthwhile or workable within the client's personality. We need, of course, to be quite clear how far the client is capable of exercising control and to what extent we need to protect ourselves and others from danger.

Here is an example of a very difficult client being skilfully handled:—Mr X. had recently been released from serving a two-year prison sentence imposed for raping his eldest daughter. A good deal of anxiety was aroused in the agency when he refused to see the male Child Care Officer and threatened to kill any member of the staff who tried to stop him getting to his children.

In the first interview with Mrs C., a Child Care Officer, he said he had been wronged. The charge that had been brought against him had been 'cooked'. The caseworker replied calmly, but firmly, that she was willing to listen to his side of the story, but that she knew that the evidence was well substantiated. She indicated that it might help if he could talk about his feelings and how these influenced his actions. That way they might together work out a different approach, so that instead of leading to the end of the relationship with his children, it might become possible in time for him to have access to them. She said that she could see him twice a week, but she could not accept violent behaviour nor could she make promises. In discussing this case with others, she felt it had been most important not to mislead him with false promises but to be honest with him and set a limited goal.

Soon the relationship with his wife became the major topic of the interviews. Mrs X. did not want to live with him any more because of his violence, but did not have the courage to face him with her decision. Mr X. arranged to meet her in the caseworker's office. In this confrontation Mrs X. said firmly that she would not have him back. Mr X. got up and took hold of his wife as if to strangle her. The worker held his wrists and told him : 'Hold on, don't act, this will not solve anything. I am not going to let you do this.' He relaxed his grip, and the worker asked Mrs X. to leave the office. Mr X. regained control and was able to express his rage in words, but threatened to attack his wife at home. The caseworker told him that if he did so, he would hurt not only his wife, but also himself. She said she was sure he could control his feelings if he thought about her as a person, and about the children, as well as his hopes for better things. She said she felt sad for him if he could not control himself, because this meant that he would again get in conflict with the law and have to go back to prison. She suggested that he get in touch with her when his feelings threatened to get out of control.

Over the next year, Mr X. came to see the caseworker at all hours and wanted to know where he could get in touch with her at any time of the day. He was never violent with her, though extremely possessive and tried to see her when no-one else was around.

On one occasion he waylaid his wife at the nursery school and pulled the youngest child, aged three, away from her. He heard the Headmistress say that she would call the police and ran away with the child, straight to the social worker's office. She asked him whether he thought this behaviour would help others to believe in him. In order to bring a case for the Court to grant him access to the children he would need to prove that he was a reasonable person. This meant caring about the child's feelings. He agreed that the child hardly knew him and it was not good for her to be dragged along by him without preparation and without the mother's consent. The caseworker got the impression that he had been kindly to the child, as the little girl did not appear unduly frightened. In the end, Mr X. himself decided that the Child Care Officer should return the child to the mother.

Gradually, this man learned to make less demands on the worker and it was sufficient for him to phone her whenever he got drunk, or felt in a violent mood. He thus used her as a parent, who cares sufficiently not to allow him to hurt others or himself. The caseworker seems to have been the container of his sane self, and her trust in a good part of him strengthened his wish to develop it. She did not provide false reassurance. Rather she challenged him to interpose thought and time between impulse and action. She thus helped him to learn to control himself, just as benevolent but firm parents realize the need to set limitations to their growing children's aggressive behaviour. We do this not only in our self-interest as individuals or members of society, but knowing that excessive destructiveness will inevitably bring in its wake punishment or excessive guilt.

We have looked at different ways in which clients may use the caseworker as a container for mental pain. In doing so, the client is expressing his need to empty these feelings into someone in the hope that the caseworker be strong and tolerant enough to be able to contain them. The caseworker acts as a kind of mother who takes away the mess that the child produces and cleans it up and helps him to do so gradually himself. This therapeutic use of the caseworker exists even when the client pours out aggressive feelings, as in the example of the rejected, angry mother. This is in fact a tribute to the caseworker's ability, and a sign of trusting her to tolerate verbal attacks without retaliating. This has to be distinguished from a really hostile relationship based on envy. The client who is looking for a good container-type relationship may heap the worker with accusations, but the envious client will make her feel that she is no good, just when she has in fact proved to be helpful.

Combining action with insight

However much we might like to avoid doing things for the client, and wish to help him to do them himself, action is called for in some cases.

A mother at breaking point

Mrs Y. arrived in a pathetic state, looking worn out and behaving in an extremely agitated manner. She said she just couldn't cope any more; her husband was ill in hospital and she had been frantically trying to look after her young family, visit her husband and keep the house in order. She burst out: 'The only thing that will help me is for you to take the children away; just for a short time, so that I can get some sleep and rest'. The worker felt herself put in a position of being given no choice, and tried to stall and find out more about this mother. The client, by now almost in tears, said desperately, 'So you won't help me, you won't do anything then'. The caseworker tried to show Mrs Y. that before they could take a decision, they should think about it a little more and consider alternatives, and also the effect the decision would have on her children. It was Mrs Y.'s degree of desperation and agitation, mixed with concern for her children's welfare which finally convinced the caseworker that this mother was at the end of her strength, and needed a respite. It was a difficult decision to make, because the children were young and might be adversely affected by the separation. On the other hand, no Home Help was available. If this distraught mother were to break down this would be a more disastrous experience for the children than being temporarily in a Children's Home. She agreed to place the children for two weeks only and arranged for the mother to take, visit and collect them from the Home. At the same time, she arranged to see her to discuss the problems which led up to her feeling so desperate.

In the event, this decision proved to be the right one. The mother made no attempt to leave the children longer than had been agreed, benefited from having the pressure of looking after them taken off her, and used the interviews with the caseworker sufficiently to be able to cope afterwards.

No money in the house
The Child Care Department was contacted by the police, because, following a disagreement over benefit payment, Mr and Mrs V. had abandoned their four-year-old child at

the local office of the Ministry of Social Security.

The office responsible for the payments told the Child Care Officer that Mr V. had been in hospital and had continued to draw benefits afterwards without supplying further medical certificates. Also he claimed not to have received two cheques sent by their office although the cheques had in fact been cashed. The Child Care Officer collected the child and returned him to the family and took the opportunity to say that leaving the child seemed to be a way of forcing the Ministry's hand as well as perhaps showing how desperate the family felt. The V.'s then told her that they had no money for food and gas-meter. They were in arrears with their rent and, as it later emerged, also with their hire purchase repayments.

This posed a dilemma for the caseworker. She suspected that she was being blackmailed and taken for a ride; if she gave them money, she would be colluding with and supporting dishonest and delinquent behaviour, and thus put herself in a position in which the V.'s would hold her in contempt. She saw her main task as finding out the reasons and feelings which had made the couple create a crisis. Nevertheless she felt that she could not begin this task until she had tided them over the present crisis, for to leave them destitute would be cruel and would be experienced by the clients as being uncaring.

The caseworker in such a situation has to tread a delicate path between on the one hand, seeming to support and be blackmailed by the destructive part of the client, and on the other hand appearing to be unconcerned if she refuses the most urgent needs for subsistence. She is likely in the one instance to be regarded as a fool who can be conned and in the other, as cruel and punitive. In both cases she might be encouraging the client to further delinquent behaviour. Furthermore, if a large sum of money were to be given, or similar situations allowed to recur, it would strengthen the client's belief that there exists an ideal mother/State whose duty it is to feed, carry or rescue the family for ever. This can lead to increased persecutory guilt because of the exploitation involved and would strengthen the client's infantile dependence.

It seemed to this particular caseworker, that however much the crisis had been engineered by the V.'s she would be right in tiding them over with a small sum so as to demonstrate her concern. At the same time she indicated that this was a temporary help only, and that her future work with the family would consist in trying to understand why they had got themselves into such a situation. At first the V.'s did not appear to co-operate. On the contrary, they assured her that Mr V. was working when in fact he was not. They also complained that the amount she gave them was inadequate and not as much as others in similar circumstances had received. However, when the caseworker combined firmness, i.e. not allowing herself to be cheated, with trying to understand the reasons for their behaviour, the situation changed. They were able to tell her that Mr V. had not gone back to his place of work and that this was because he was afraid that others would find out about his deafness and ridicule him.

It seems that Mr V. found it easier to present himself as someone incapable of managing his external affairs rather than face the feelings of inferiority and persecution. The caseworker was able eventually to get through to these feelings, partly because she indicated that she was concerned to understand. At first, as we have seen, she also held the projective feelings of being helpless, i.e. *she* felt inadequate, because she had been put into the situation by the client of being wrong whatever she did. At the same time, she demonstrated that there were more constructive ways of dealing with helplessness than being either dishonest or adopting an 'I don't care' attitude. This seems to have made it possible for Mr V. to face his real problems with her more honestly, to admit to feelings of

inadequacy and fear of ridicule. Once his infantile feelings had been understood and been listened to with
sympathy by the caseworker he was able to make some
constructive plans for the future. He got himself a hearing aid and found a job in which his deafness did not
interfere with his ability to work.

Considerations governing active intervention and the case-
worker's behaviour

By the very nature of her work, the caseworker often finds
herself, as in the two cases above, having to take an
active role. The difficulty would seem to lie precisely in
(a) knowing when to resist such active intervention, however much one might be pressed into it; (b) using one's
insight to resist acting without prior consideration of
the feelings involved and (c) being aware how the worker's
action will affect the client's phantasies about himself and
the worker.

The particular skill of the social worker seems to me to
lie in having to make such difficult decisions and, in some
cases, combining the exploration of feelings and emotional
pain with having to take action. It is important to strive
to do as little as possible, for any active intervention tends
to infantilize the client, lead to inertia, to resentment
and persecution as well as to promote despair about not
being able to cope oneself. The worker has constantly to
sort out whether she is being manipulated, drawn into
fitting in with the unrealistic wishes of the client, colluding with his destructive parts, and/or helping him to avoid
facing inner conflicts by externalizing his problems. In all
these instances, she would not be helping the client to
cope with anxiety and would undermine the struggle
towards growth.

At other times, however, she may come to the conclusion that the client is overwhelmed and really unable
to cope, has lost control or might damage himself or
others, and that it is therefore appropriate for her to

intervene. Or the client may be so infantile in his development and have had so little opportunity to experience maternal understanding, that the first demonstration of concern has to be through material aid. However, one would hope that this would only be a temporary measure.

Much of social work is bound up with fulfilling statutory obligations and having to help clients to make or accept decisions made on their behalf. In all these instances the prime concern is to understand and help the client with his feelings. But the client's awareness of the caseworker's powerful position may in those instances work against frank discussion. For instance, the Child Care Officer's report on the prospective parents will decide whether they will receive a child for adoption. The report which the Probation Officer gives to the Court, can tip the balance between punishment, placement in an Approved School or prison, and probation. Similarly, some caseworkers are known to hold the purse or be in the position to urge others to open theirs, or provide other material help. All these circumstances may drive the clients to present themselves in a good light, to be the 'good deserving poor' and suppress information and emotions which would in their opinion prejudice her against them. This makes the caseworker's task of assessing what their real needs are and how they can best be helped, a more difficult one. She needs to consider carefully what the anxieties are against which the client is defending himself; sometimes in order to make the right decision, at other times in order to be able to help him carry or face anxieties.

Due consideration in terms of what it may mean to the client must be given to such questions as giving advice, accepting gifts, answering questions about her private life, and having physical contact with children. For example, we would, before we give advice, wonder whether this is really helpful and whether, on the basis of this client's past record, he was able to use advice constructively. In accepting gifts, we would want to know in our mind whether these are little tokens of appreciation, or a sign of vying with a giving mother/worker or trying to be a 'special' client; or a sign of avoiding depression by omnipotent reparation; or a means of seducing the worker. It is really difficult to tackle someone's even quite blatant feelings of aggression when they have just given you a present! It may be natural to comfort a child by physically holding him and this has to be distinguished from trying to seduce him and prevent him from airing grievances or experiencing depression. All these situations require to be handled with tact and understanding based on informed intuition. For within the limits imposed by professional conduct, it is most important to be oneself.

3

Some thoughts on the responsibility and burden of casework

Extent and limits of responsibility

Caseworkers sometimes find it difficult to believe that they occupy such an extremely important place in the client's mental life, especially when a client does not appear to value the contact. This is misplaced modesty, for this important position of the caseworker owes, at least at the beginning of the relationship, little to the worker's ability. It is derived from the wealth of feelings which the client brings into the relationship with the professional helper.

We have seen that these feelings reach into the depth of infantile fears and hopes. By virtue of offering a service, the caseworker is thus accepting from the start of the contact with the client a position of trust, and this imposes on her a grave responsibility. Her attitude and handling may provide the client with the opportunity for a new and different experience which increases his realistic hopes and gives constructive drives a chance to develop; or else it might be just another disappointing experience which confirms old suspicions, shatters hope and ends in greater despair and a strengthening of his defensive system. Every experience becomes part of the internal equipment influencing the next stage. Failure to respond to the client's real, though often unconscious needs, may lead to an increase in hopelessness and fear, thus making it more difficult for him to seek help subsequently.

The caseworker may not be able to pick up the most pressing anxieties of the client at any particular moment of time. What is essential to the client is the caseworker's willingness to *try* to understand how he feels, to be prepared to listen and respect him as a unique personality. Her actions, as well as her words, will show the client whether she is really concerned about him and in touch with the adult and infantile parts of his personality and whether she has the courage and integrity to face emotional pain. Abilities in this direction are of as much, if not more, importance to the client than her technical skill, though ideally, of course, they will all go together.

In our behaviour with clients we must be alive to the fact that we are dealing with a highly dynamic situation and that what we do and say is interpreted by the client in terms of his infantile phantasies as well as his more adult rational self. We have seen the vulnerability of the infant and child and the infantile parts of the personality; the wish for an ideal relationship out of fear of persecution and terror; the ease with which the 'ideal' turns into its opposite when unrealistic hopes are disappointed; mistrust due, amongst other things, to envious devaluation and often increased by bad experiences; the ease with which hostility can be evoked and the fear that this will shatter the good relationship. For all these reasons the client is emotionally dependent, frightened and worried at the reaction, and even the survival, of the worker.

It is, therefore, of the utmost importance that the caseworker show herself to be reliable and trustworthy and so avoid causing unnecessary pain. It becomes, for instance, essential to be in the right place at the appointed time. We should refrain from cancelling appointments lightly. We should try to shield the client from unnecessary stimulation of jealousy and envy by keeping our private life, and activities with other clients, from intruding into our relationship with him.

Holidays handing over and ending a relationship

become major issues which require many weeks, if not months, of preparation. It is not enough simply to mention a forthcoming separation. One has to keep it in mind and not allow the client to deny or underestimate what the break may mean to him. While much has been written about the ill-effects of separation on children, the intensity of the adult's reactions have in the past often been disregarded, because the infantile part of the adult personality has not been sufficiently taken into account. Feelings of mistrust of the worker, attempts to devalue the relationship, anger at being let down, fear of having been too greedy or caused actual harm, sadness about loss, the painfulness of pining for the relationship—these are but some of the feelings that may be involved. The client's mental stability during the worker's temporary absence, his ability to transfer and his continued well-being at the end of the contact depend largely on the work done on feelings surrounding loss. These matters have in the past usually been given insufficient attention. This may be due to a lack of understanding of the depth and richness of feelings and phantasies. Another reason in the case of a transfer may be that the worker's possessiveness of her client and her jealousy and envy of her successor interfere with adequately preparing the client. Perhaps the most important obstacle is the caseworker's wish to avoid the full impact of feelings of guilt and depression at leaving her client. This tends to result on the one hand in postponing telling the client, or doing so only in passing, and on the other hand, in the shifting of the responsibility for the continued welfare of the client on to the agency. It is of course important to the client that there exist other caseworkers who will carry on, just as it is comforting to a child whose mother goes away that there is a father and a wider family to look after him. But the uniqueness of the particular person and the feelings attached to her make the loss a very frightening and very painful event. If the child/adult is inadequately prepared to deal with loss, not only is the preservation of this particular relationship internally threatened, but also his capacity to relate to other members of the family/agency may be so impaired that he will just not give them a chance.

While the caseworker is responsible for providing the best service she is capable of, she is not responsible for the client's improvement. If things do not go well, she will of course wish to examine carefully whether and where she went wrong. But perhaps it is helpful for the caseworker to remind herself that she is responsible only for providing a specific service as part of an environment that enables growth and development to take place and *not* for the client's ability to make use of it. We have seen, for instance, (in the chapter on envy) that, as the proverb says, 'One can take a horse to the water, but cannot make it drink'. The client's ability to benefit from the relationship depends, in part, on his inborn capacities and in part on his ability to recover his best potential after perhaps many terrible experiences. Even with help over a long period he may be unable to get in touch with feelings which disturb his relationship with himself and others; either because of an intolerance to frustration, or, having lacked the experience of a relationship in which his anxieties could be held, he has built up such rigid or massive defences against emotional pain that he no longer dares to give them up.

There is a point at which it is therapeutic to interrupt or end a contact that has become sterile. It should be openly stated that it appears that the client can go no further at the present and the door left open for the client to return. Alternatively, one may have to admit failure, either because this particular caseworker is unable to deal with this particular client, or because the kind of help she offers is not the appropriate one; alternative arrangements may have to be considered.

Finally, we must bear in mind that we are not omniscient or omnipotent and that with our present knowledge and facilities we may be as yet inadequately equipped to help certain kinds of clients.

The burden of casework and some safeguards

Pressures converge on the caseworker from many different directions. There is the pressure from o her agencies or some authority that the caseworker find a solution, 'fix up' the client in some way or other for the moment, irrespective of the long-term effects. There is the pressure from society that the caseworker relieve it from the responsibility of taking a share in carrying its weaker and more difficult members. There is the pressure from clients to be given a life free of pain. But the pressures that are the hardest to resist and which make her so open to other people's unreasonable demands, come from within the caseworker herself. It is the demand from within that she be omnipotently reparative, rescue the poor, the ill, the damaged, the underprivileged.

We have seen that even when all unreasonable pressures can be resisted, the appropriate burden of casework is an extremely heavy one: it is *making oneself available* to the client's excessive emotional pain and holding or carrying it for him for a period of time. The possibility of the strain becoming too great, resulting in having to give up her job or having a break-down or else protecting herself against pain by becoming more superficial, dogmatic and rigid, is one that needs to be taken seriously.

There are certain safeguards which at present do not seem to me to receive sufficient attention. One is the need for more regulated free time, especially in the evenings, so that the worker has an opportunity for recreation and enrichment in social life and hobbies. The second is the recognition of the caseworker's limits. Each person will find that there are some clients they can deal with, and that some others impose too great a strain. Thirdly, more professional help is needed, particularly from those psychiatrists who have sympathy for and understanding of the problems of social workers. Lastly, the importance of supervision cannot be over-estimated. It would seem essential, not only for the beginner, but also more senior staff. It is important in the first place because it is a way of sharing the heavy responsibility and anxieties aroused in the course of the work; it is a check against distortion due to personal problems; it is a way of counteracting getting into a rut and it provides an opportunity for learning, to develop and further one's insight and skill.

While liaison with colleagues working on the same case is important in its own right, it is an inappropriate forum for the discussion of the caseworker's personal difficulties with the client. There is the danger that colleagues will either join in criticizing the client or that the competition between them may lead to disagreement and deterioration in the working relationship. It is far preferable that the caseworker discuss the case with someone not directly concerned, either inside or outside the agency so that she can approach her colleagues not from a position of weakness, but with knowledge based on insight and understanding.

Such understanding implies that the caseworker does not need to deny the problems (nor strengths) of her clients, nor those of the social set-up in which they find themselves. Knowing that she is not omnipotent, she will sometimes wish to refer cases for other professional help.

She may also become aware of the need for social change where the environment causes unnecessary suffering or hinders emotional growth. She may be in the position, on the strength of her knowledge and experience, to draw attention to the need for such changes in the social services, care-giving institutions and the training of personnel working in them. She must bear in mind, however, that those in responsible positions are human beings beset by the same kind of conflicts, anxieties and defences against them as we have been discussing throughout this book.

Suggestions for further reading

I have selected those writings by Sigmund Freud and Melanie Klein which form a useful introduction to their work or are of special interest to social workers. I shall suggest relevant writings by Kleinian analysts and have included a few by other psycho-analysts as well as some papers by caseworkers whose approach is psycho-analytically orientated.

I have added no comments where the subject matter is self-evident from the title.

On child development

BICK, E., 'Notes on Infant Observation' (1964) A discussion of the value and difficulty of observing babies. Written by Kleinian psycho-analyst.

'Child Analysis Today' (1962) Although this paper is addressed to psycho-analysts I recommend it to caseworkers because it explores the feelings aroused in those who work with children.

KLEIN, M., 'On Observing The Behaviour of Young Infants' (1952) Descriptive and analytic study of 0-1 year olds.

HARRIS, M., OSBORNE, E., O'SHAUNESSY, E., ROSENBLUTH, D., and others. *Your . . . Year Old* (1969) Booklets each covering emotional development of a particular age-group, from infancy to late adolescence. Written by child psychotherapists, a child psychologist and a child psychiatrist of the Tavistock Clinic. (Not in print in 1985.)

HARRIS, M., *Thinking about Infants and Young Children* (1975).

MEYERS, S., (ed.), *Adolescence: The Crisis of Adjustment* (1975), *Adolescence and Breakdown* (1975) Studies of adolescents by members of the Tavistock Clinic and other British experts.

WINNICOTT, D. W., *The Child, The Family and The Outside World* (1964) Based on talks to mothers. Deals mainly with mother's feelings about the baby and the baby's experience of his world. Also with some problems of older children. *The Maturational Process and the Facilitating Environment* (1965) Studies in the theory of emotional development.

On psychosis: writings by Kleinian psycho-analysts

BION, W. R., 'Differentiation of the Psychotic from the Non-Psychotic Part of the Personality' (1957).

'Attacks on Linking' (1959) An analysis of a particular disturbance in thinking.

MELTZER, D., BREMNER, J., HOXTER, S. H., WEDDELL, D., and WITTENBERG, I., 'Explorations in Autism: A Psycho-Analytical Study' (1975).

ROSENFELD, H. A., Three papers in the Book *Psychotic States* (1965) Deals with the psycho-pathology and analysis of psychotic conditions. 'Notes on the Super-Ego Conflict in an Acute Schizophrenic'. 'Transference Phenomena in an Acute Schizophrenic Patient'. 'Psychopathology and Psycho-Analytic Treatment of Schizophrenia'.

SEGAL, H., 'Psychopathology of Paranoid Schizoid Position', from *Introduction to the Work of Melanie Klein* (1964) This deals with abnormal development in the paranoid schizoid position and its relation to a paranoid personality structure.

SUGGESTIONS FOR FURTHER READING

On groups: writings by Kleinian psycho-analysts

BION, W. R., *Experiences in Groups* (1961) On group tensions, group dynamics and basic unconscious assumptions made by groups. Though mainly based on work with therapeutic groups, the findings are of great relevance to other group situations and social institutions.

GOSLING, R., and TURQUET, P. M., 'The Training of General Practitioners' (1967) Recommended for its study of group dynamics and particularly for the use of the group for teaching purposes.

On various specific topics papers: by Kleinian psycho-analysts

GOSLING, R., *What is Transference?* (1968) Based on a public lecture. It sums up the importance of transference and takes a look at the history of the concept.

HARRIS, M., and CARR, H., 'Therapeutic Consultations' (1966) Two papers on joint consultations with parents and children. Mrs Harris gives details of interviews with parents showing how they were helped to find a better solution themselves to their child's problem. Miss Carr brings details of two interviews with a child in mother's presence.

JACQUES, E., *Death and the Mid-Life Crisis* (1965) A paper dealing with the change of outlook which takes place in middle age and relating it to the working through of the depressive position.

'Guilt, Conscience and Social Behaviour' (1968) Based on a public lecture.

KLEIN, M., 'On Criminality' (1934) Shows its relationship to mental structure, i.e. having introjected severe internal parents.

ROSENFELD, H. A., *Drug-Addiction*. In: *Psychotic States* (1965) Psycho-pathology of the Drug Addict.

WILLIAMS, A. H., 'The Treatment of Abnormal Murderers' (1965) Psycho-pathology of murderers as seen in the course of analysing them.

Psycho-analytic insight applied to casework

ASSOCIATION OF PSYCHIATRIC SOCIAL WORKERS, *Relationship in Casework* (1964) A number of short papers dealing with the different aspects of the subject.

INSTITUTE OF MARITAL STUDIES, *The Marital Relationship as a Focus for Casework* (1962) A useful introduction to the work and approach developed by the Family Discussion Bureau.

FERARD, M. L. and HUNNYBUN, N. K., *The Caseworker's Use of Relationship* (1962) Written some years ago, it is still probably the most helpful introduction to the subject.

HUTTEN, J. M., 'Short-Term Contracts in Social Work' (1977).

IRVINE, E. E., 'Psychosis in Parents' and 'Mental Illness as a Problem for the Family' (1961/2) Short papers on the anxieties of the family of the mentally ill.

MATTINSON, J., and SINCLAIR, I., 'Mate and Stalemate: Working with Marital Problems in a Social Services Department' (1979).

PINCUS, L., 'Death and the Family: The Importance of Mourning' (1976).

WINNICOTT, C., 'Face to Face with Children' (1963) The paper shows how flexible the caseworker needs to be in working with children and shows some of the difficulties she may encounter.

WINNICOTT, D. W., *The Mentally Ill in Your Caseload* (1963) Written for social workers and appreciative of the heavy burden they carry.

Psycho-analytic insight applied to related problems

BOWLBY, J., *Forty-four Juvenile Thieves and their Character and Home Life* (1946) Pathology is related to separation at an early age.

Child Care and the Growth of Love (1953) Discusses the need for continued maternal care and gives details about Dr Bowlby's and other researchers' work on separation anxieties.

MATTINSON, J., 'The Reflective Process in Casework Supervision' (1975).

MENZIES, I., *A Case Study in the Functioning of Social Systems* (1960) A Report on Nursing Service. A Kleinian psycho-analyst looks at the anxiety and defences aroused in nurses and how these are embodied in the structure of the service.

MILLER, D. H., *Growth to Freedom* (1964) Psychological Treatment of Delinquents. Particularly useful in showing how analytical knowledge can help in the setting up of a therapeutic community.

ROBERTSON, J., *Young Children in Hospital* (1958) A short introduction to the work on separation anxiety of the analyst best known for his films of children in hospital.

Applied psycho-analysis: topics of general interest

FREUD, S., *Psychopathology of Everyday Life* (1901) Unconscious motivation as it is shown in forgetting, misreading, making slips of the tongue etc.

KLEIN, M., 'Some Reflections on the "Oresteia"' (From *Our Adult World and its Roots in Infancy*) A psycho-analytical study of the trilogy of Aeschylus.

MONEY-KYRLE, R. E., *Man's Picture of his World* (1961) Making many links between psycho-analysis, and other sciences, and showing the application of psycho-analysis to social issues; particularly recommended are:
Chapter 1: The Nature of the Evidence.
         8: On Ethics.
        10: On Avoidable Sources of Conflict.
        11: On Political Philosophies.

SEGAL, H., 'A Psycho-analytic Approach to Aesthetics' (1956) Discusses what makes artists produce satisfactory work and what elements make for satisfactory aesthetic experience.

STOKES, A. and MELTZER, D., *Painting and the Inner World* (1963) A. Stokes reflects on the work of Turner in the light of analytic knowledge. Includes a dialogue with D. Meltzer, Kleinian analyst, on the social basis of art and how it is related to the depressive position.

Additional reading of S. Freud and M. Klein's work and an introduction to Klein's work

Books not mentioned under previous headings
Those marked with * are short papers.

FREUD, S., *On the History of the Psycho-Analytic Movement** (1914).

The Question of Lay Analysis* (1926) In this paper Freud has an imaginary conversation with 'An Impartial Observer' and so the chance to explain and answer questions about psycho-analytic treatment.

Analysis of a Phobia in a Five-Year-old Boy* (1909).

Beyond the Pleasure Principle* (1920) Meta psychology; about the Life and Death Instinct and how Freud arrived at this concept.

The Interpretation of Dreams (1900).

KLEIN, M., *Our Adult World and its Roots in Infancy* (1963) Psycho-analytic approach to the study of our society.

Envy and Gratitude (1957) Psycho-analytic study including clinical illustrations.

'On Identification'* (1955) Explains projective identification by studying the Julian Green novel *If I were you.*

'On the Sense of Loneliness'* (1963) A profound study of factors which contribute to our feeling lonely.

KLEIN, M. and RIVIERE, J., *Love, Hate and Reparation* (1937) Relating our social behaviour to the conflict between love and hate.

MELTZER, D., 'The Kleinian Development' (1978) This is a chronological and critical review of the contributions of Freud, Klein and Bion to our model of the mind.

SEGAL, H., *Introduction to the Work of Melanie Klein* (1973) Based on a series of lectures given to students of psycho-analysis and introducing them to Klein's psycho-analytic theory and practice. Includes many clinical illustrations.

Bibliography

This bibliography does not cover *all* the writings of S. Freud and M. Klein on which this book is based. I have listed only those which are specifically referred to in the text.

ABRAHAM, K., (1924) *A short Study of the Development of the Libido Viewed in the Light of Mental Disorders*, Selected Papers of Karl Abraham, Hogarth Press.

ASSOCIATION OF PSYCHIATRIC SOCIAL WORKERS, (1964) *Relationship in Casework*, Assoc. of Psychiatric Social Workers.

BICK, E., (1962) 'Child Analysis Today', *International Journal of Psycho-Analysis*, Vol. 43.

(1964) 'Notes on Infant Observation in Psycho-analytic Training', *International Journal of Psycho-Analysis*, Vol. 45.

BION, W. R., (1957) 'Differentiation of the Psychotic from the Non-Psychotic Part of the Personality', *International Journal of Psycho-Analysis*, Vol. 38.

(1959) 'Attacks on Linking', *International Journal of Psycho-Analysis*, Vol. 40.

(1961) *Experience in Groups*, Tavistock Publications.

(1962) *Learning from Experience*, Heinemann.

BOWLBY, J., (1946) *Forty-four Juvenile Thieves and their Character and Home Life*, Baillière, Tindall & Cassell. (1953) *Child Care and the Growth of Love*, Penguin.

BREUER, J. and FREUD, S., (1893-5) *Studies on Hysteria*, Standard Ed. of the Complete Psychological Works of S. Freud, Vol. 2, Hogarth Press.

FAMILY DISCUSSION BUREAU, (1962) *The Marital Relationship as a Focus for Casework*, Hitchin: Codicote Press.

FERARD, M. L. and HUNNYBUN, N. K., (1962) *The Caseworker's Use of Relationship*, Mind & Medicine Monographs.

FREUD, S., (1895) *Psychotherapy of Hysteria*, Standard Ed. of the Complete Psychological Works of S. Freud, Vol. 2, Hogarth Press.

(1900) *The Interpretation of Dreams*, Standard Ed. Vols. 4 and 5.

(1901) *The Psychopathology of Everyday Life*, Standard Ed. Vol. 6.

(1905) *Fragments of an Analysis of a Case of Hysteria*, Standard Ed. Vol. 7.

(1909) *Analysis of a Phobia in a Five-Year-Old Boy*, Standard Ed. Vol. 10.

(1914) *On the History of the Psycho-Analytic Movement*, Standard Ed. Vol. 14.

(1917) *Mourning and Melancholia*, Standard Ed. Vol. 14.

(1920) *Beyond the Pleasure Principle*, Standard Ed. Vol. 18.

(1923) *The Ego and the Superego*, Standard Ed. Vol. 19.

(1926) *The Question of Lay Analysis*, Standard Ed. Vol. 20.

(1933) Femininity, in *New Introductory Lectures*, Standard Ed. Vol. 22.

GOSLING, R., (1968) *What is Transference? The Psychoanalytic Approach*, Baillière, Tindall & Cassell.

GOSLING, R. and TURQUET, P. M., (1967) The Training of General Practitioners in *The Use of Small Groups in*

    Training, Hitchin: Codicote Press.

HARRIS, M. and CARR, H., (1966) 'Therapeutic Consultations', *Journal of Child Psychotherapy*, Vol. 1, No. 4, Association of Child Psychotherapists (Non-Medical).

HARRIS, M., OSBORNE, E., O'SHAUNESSY, E., ROSENBLUTH, D., and others., (1969) *Your ... Year Old*, a series of paperbacks on year by year child development, Transworld Publications.

HARRIS, M., (1969) *Inside Information on Understanding Infants*, Dickins Press.

IRVINE, E. E., (1961/62) 'Psychosis in Parents' and 'Mental Illness as a Problem for the Family', *British Journal of Psychiatric Social Work*, Vol. 6.

ISAACS, S., (1952) 'The Nature and Function of Phantasy' in *Developments in Psycho-Analysis*, Hogarth Press.

JACQUES, E., (1965) 'Death and the Mid-Life Crisis', *International Journal of Psycho-Analysis*, Vol. 46.

    (1968) 'Guilt, Conscience and Social Behaviour', in *The Psychoanalytic Approach*, Baillière, Tindall & Cassell.

KLEIN, M., (1926) 'The Psychological Foundations of Child Analysis', in *Psychoanalysis of Children*, Hogarth Press.

    (1928) 'Early Stages of the Oedipus Conflict and of Super-Ego Formation', in *Psychoanalysis of Children*, Hogarth Press.

    (1933) 'The Early Development of Conscience in the Child', in *Contributions to Psycho-Analysis*, Hogarth Press.

    (1934) 'On Criminality', in *Contributions to Psycho-Analysis*, Hogarth Press.

    (1935) 'A Contribution to the Psychogenesis of Manic Depressive States', in *Contributions to Psycho-Analysis*, Hogarth Press.

    (1940) 'Mourning—Its Relation to Manic-Depressive States', in *Contributions to Psycho-Analysis*, Hogarth Press.

(1946) 'Notes on Some Schizoid Mechanisms', in *Developments in Psycho-Analysis*, Hogarth Press.

(1948) 'On the Theory of Anxiety and Guilt', in *Developments in Psycho-Analysis*, Hogarth Press.

(1952) 'On Observing the Behaviour of Young Infants', in *Developments in Psycho-Analysis*, Hogarth Press.

(1955) 'On Identification' in *New Directions in Psycho-Analysis*, also in *Our Adult World and Its Roots in Infancy*, Hogarth Press. (See ref. below.)

(1957) *Envy and Gratitude*, Tavistock Publications.

(1963) 'On the Sense of Loneliness', in *Our Adult World and Its Roots in Infancy*. (See below.)

(1963) *Our Adult World and Its Roots in Infancy and other Essays*, Heinemann.

KLEIN, M. and RIVIERE, J., (1937) *Love, Hate and Reparation*, Hogarth Press.

MELTZER, D. and STOKES, A., (1963) 'Concerning the Social Basis of Art', in *Painting and the Inner World*, Tavistock Publications.

MENZIES, I., (1960) 'A Case Study in the Functioning of Social Systems as a Defence Against Anxiety', (A Report on a Study of the Nursing Service of a General Hospital), *Human Relations Journal*, Vol. 13, No. 2.

MIDDLEMORE, H. P., (1941) *The Nursing Couple*, Hamish Hamilton.

MILLER, D. H., (1964) *Growth to Freedom*, Tavistock Publications.

MONEY-KYRLE, R. E., (1961) *Man's Picture of his World*, Duckworth.

ROBERTSON, J., (1958) *Young Children in Hospital*, Tavistock Publications.

ROSENFELD, H. A., (1962) 'The Super-Ego and the Ego Ideal', *International Journal of Psycho-Analysis*, Vol. 43.

(1965) *Psychotic States: A Psycho-Analytical Approach*, Hogarth Press and Institute of Psycho-Analysis.

SEGAL, H., (1956) 'A Psycho-analytic Approach to Aesthetics', *International Journal of Psycho-Analysis*, Vol. 33.

(1958) 'Fear of Death: Notes on the Analysis of an Old Man', *International Journal of Psycho-Analysis*, Vol. 39.

(1964) *Introduction to the Work of Melanie Klein*, Heinemann.

SPITZ, R., (1945) 'Hospitalism', *Psychoanalytic Study of the Child*, Vol. 1.

STEVENSON, O., (1963) 'Skills in Supervision', *in New Thinking for Changing Needs*, Association of Social Workers.

STOKES, A., (1963) *Painting and the Inner World*, Tavistock Publications.

WILLIAMS, A. N., (1965) 'The Treatment of Abnormal Murderers', *Howard Journal of Penology*, Vol. 2.

WINNICOTT, C., (1963) 'Face to Face with Children', in *New Thinking for Changing Needs*, Association of Social Workers.

WINNICOTT, D. W., (1955) 'The Depressive Position in Normal Emotional Development', *British Journal of Medical Psychology*, Vol. 28.

(1963) 'The Mentally Ill in Your Caseload', in *New Thinking for Changing Needs*, Association of Social Workers.

(1964) *The Child, The Family and the Outside World*, Penguin.

(1965) *The Maturational Process and the Facilitating Environment*, Hogarth Press.